THE
FUTURE
of
EGYPTOLOGY

THE
FUTURE
of
EGYPTOLOGY

Monica Hanna

MELVILLE HOUSE UK

LONDON

THE FUTURE of EGYPTOLOGY

First published in 2025 by
Melville House UK
Suite 2000
16/18 Woodford Road
London E7 0HA

and

Melville House Publishing
46 John Street
Brooklyn, NY 11200I

mhpbooks.com @melvillehouse

A CIP catalogue record for this book is available from the British Library

UK: 978-1-911545-73-6
US: 978-1-685891-63-3

1 3 5 7 9 10 8 6 4 2

Printed in Denmark by Nørhaven, Viborg
Typesetting by Roland Codd

To Maya

What the pyramid hid is empty
See now, the land is deprived of kingship
By a few people who ignore custom
See now, men rebel against the Serpent
(Stolen) is the crown of Re, who pacifies
the Two Lands
If the resident is stripped, it will collapse
in a moment.
The secrets of Egypt's kings are bared.
Men stir up strife unopposed
See, the land is tied up in gangs

The Admonitions of Ipuwer[1]

---

1. (Lichtheim 1973), 156.

Introduction

My fascination with ancient Egypt began with the beautiful stories and songs my grandmother's housekeeper used to recount to us during school vacations at our family house in Minya. We called her 'Naema', and although her tales bore echoes of the ancient world, their meaning was, to my childhood self, tantalisingly unclear. One rhyme she used to sing was 'Ya Talea al-Shagara, Hatly Maak Baa'ara', which in literal translation means calling for 'the man going up the tree to bring down the cow' – a phrase I later encountered during my BA in Egyptology at the American University in Cairo. Professor Fayza Haikal would relate this song to the changing of religions that took place in Egypt, from paganism to Christianity to Islam; the 'cow in the tree' represented

Hathor, an ancient goddess and the subject of worship in my country thousands of years ago.

I hated social studies classes at school; they were presented to us in the general Egyptian curriculum as dry, fragmented, and focused on memorising facts for exams. Yet, there were moments that pointed to my ultimate direction. My school, Ramses College for Girls (previously the American College for Girls), took us on a trip to the Cairo Museum in the first year of high school. I remember marvelling at the colossal statues of Akhenaten, and while I wandered around the rest of the museum, fascinated by every object, I saw a sign reading 'Mummification Lab'. Ever the curious student, I snuck behind the sign and peeked at what was happening there. I saw three figures – whom I would later discover were Dr Nasry Iskander, Ms Marwa el-Zeiny and the late Madame Omaima Mohamed – standing over a mummy, released from its case. They spotted me and, instead of shooing me from the room, beckoned me over to look: they were conserving the feet of Tuthmosis III, whose toes had fallen off. They were putting the bones back in place so that he could experience eternity with his feet pointing in the right direction. I crept up slowly until I was face to face with him, with not a glass barrier in sight. I think it was then I fell in love with the Cairo Museum, and with Egyptology as a whole. I began volunteering after school at the lab, where I was allowed to clean the conservation materials, or to type important notes on my computer at home and bring them printed for Dr Iskander.

I went on to excel in mathematics and science, so I studied to become an engineer – yet I continued to volunteer at the mummification lab. One summer, I was writing a paper for one of the freshmen writing courses at university, and I chose a topic related to ancient Egypt. My mother told me that I should switch my subject to Egyptology and do something that I truly loved. That was enough to convince me. The next day, I changed my major and never looked back. On the contrary, I fell in love with studying the different courses; with being at the Cairo Museum as often as I wanted. I still remember sitting in room 203 of the Rare Books Library, watching the beautiful art and architecture slides, and spending hours fiddling with a Middle Egyptian assignment. The best such times were the field trips to the various archaeological sites in Egypt, particularly those off the beaten track. I also volunteered for many archaeological missions where I picked up plenty of skills – as well as observing first-hand much of what I have written about in this book.

I went on to graduate school and received a PhD in Archaeology from the University of Pisa in Italy. It was just a few months later, in 2011, that revolution swept through Egypt, with thousands of Egyptians taking to the streets asking for 'Bread, Freedom and Social Justice'. Although I was not in Cairo at the time, I could not stop thinking about what might happen at the city's many archaeological sites during the tumult. I remember receiving phone calls from the site inspectors where I had worked asking for help because of rampant looting. But I was stuck in Italy, and all I had was Facebook and Twitter. I started writing and posting about the reports I was getting and, once flights to Egypt resumed, I returned as soon as possible. Then, instead of simply receiving reports, I was able to visit the sites to compose them myself, and to photograph the looting and land grabbing – which was indeed extensive, with thousands of objects being pillaged. My social media posts received national and international media attention.

Then, in August 2013, during further political upheaval in Egypt, I experienced a disaster closer to home: the Mallawi Museum in my hometown was attacked and ransacked, following three days of clashes during which a member of the museum staff was shot and killed. Shortly afterwards, I received a phone call from a high-ranking employee at the Ministry of Antiquities asking me for images of the looted museum, and so I travelled there from Cairo with a friend of mine, the *al-Masry al-Youm* reporter Safa Allam. The Mallawi Museum resembled a war zone – and while I was still inside taking photographs, a young boy came in and started destroying some of the remaining glass cases and artefacts. I asked him what he was doing, and he told me that they belonged to the government. He was angry at the government, so he wanted to take revenge on the museum.

This was a true eye-opener for me. Despite the many community archaeology projects I have worked with, Egyptology itself seemed to have failed on some basic level; here was living proof of its failure. I communicated with the Ministry of Antiquities in Cairo about what happened; that there were still antiquities lying around the museum that could have easily been stolen or destroyed. The following day, we returned with the Antiquities Police and salvaged around forty-five of the original 1,089 objects in the museum. After clearing the museum for three days, I returned to Cairo and finally cried like I had never cried before.

Besides witnessing the destruction and being in the crossfire, the interaction with that young boy

taking revenge over his heritage made me realise that
there is something very wrong with Egyptology. All
at once, I saw a different image of the looting I had
been documenting. The veil, it seems, had fallen from
the fascination with 'wonderful things', as Howard
Carter said when he opened Tutankhamun's tomb.
Instead, the time had come to reflect on the inherent racism and social inequality in the discipline; the
colonialism, post-colonialism and imperialism that
has shaped Egyptology for two hundred years. What
had led to this boy not just to loot, but also to *destroy*
parts of the museum where, in another life, he might
have been taking part in a weekend workshop?

Since that moment, I have been writing, speak-
ing publicly, and teaching about Egyptology's many
wrongs, in the hope that it will change someday to
become a more relevant, meaningful and decolonised
discipline. This gradual process frequently elicits
antagonism, especially on issues of restitution or
repatriation. For some, I have become a protagonist;
for many others, I am the official disturber of the peace.
This book is an attempt to deconstruct Egyptology
by addressing its difficult heritage, current theory and
praxis, and offering ideas for its transformation.

Glossary of Terms

Anastylosis The word is derived from the Ancient Greek words 'στηλόω' (*stylō*), which means 'to erect', and 'ανα' (*ana*), which means 'again'. It entails meticulously locating and piecing together a structure's original components like a giant jigsaw puzzle. Additional materials might be added for stability but should be easily distinguished from the originals.

Concession In the context of archaeology, a formal agreement that grants permission to excavate and study a specific archaeological site.

Deconstruction A critical approach developed by the French philosopher Jacques Derrida to challenge traditional ideas about meaning through analysing hidden assumptions and power dynamics within texts and social structures. Deconstruction opposes binary oppositions such as good/evil; reason/emotion; and darkness/light, showing that such fixed categories are unstable, and that by using deconstruction as a thought process a more nuanced understanding of the past and present can be created.

Fellahin A plural term that refers to peasant farmers or agricultural labourers in Arab countries. It comes from the singular form 'fellah', which translates to 'ploughman' or 'tiller' in Arabic. It differentiated such members of society, particularly in the nineteenth and twentieth centuries, from the Effendiya, who were educated and worked in different government offices.

Firman A historical term referring to an official decree, order, licence or grant issued by a ruler, a viceroy or a sultan in the Ottoman state.

Historiography A discipline focusing on how history is interpreted and written. It requires more than the memorising of dates; it requires analysis of the sources, techniques and viewpoints that historians employ. It poses queries such as: Why do we prioritise some occurrences above others? What effects do political and social environments have on the way history is interpreted? By looking at these issues, historiography helps us develop a more critical and nuanced view of the past.

Phenomenology is the study of diverse phenomena as they present themselves through an individual's direct awareness and experience. It focuses on perception rather than socio-historical analysis. It mainly focuses on people's lived experiences of a phenomenon and how it feels for those who go through that experience. It is a less common method for the social sciences than anthropological ethnographic practice, which attempts to understand a group of people's worlds and 'see' the same issues that the group sees to make sense of their world.

Post-Processual Archaeology The 1980s posed a challenge to processual archaeology's scientific orientation. It made the case that locations and artefacts are more than merely bits of information. According to post-processualists, these remnants have symbolic meaning and were understood in a variety of ways by earlier societies. They explore social concerns such as identity and power, noting that the historical record may have a bias in favour of the powerful. By combining feminist, Marxist and post-colonialist theories, this method promotes a diversity of viewpoints. It helps comprehend the past as a complex web of experiences and interpretations rather than merely as a succession of historical facts.

Processual Archaeology Sometimes referred to as new archaeology, a movement emerging in the 1960s and 1970s that attempted to use a scientific perspective to transform archaeology. Processual archaeologists employed statistics and data analysis instead of merely gathering artefacts to comprehend the workings of historical societies. They examined these cultures' social structures, economic management and environmental adaptations, viewing them as intricate systems. The way that historical cultures changed and evolved was made clearer by this emphasis on cultural ecology. A more theoretical and scientific understanding of the past was made possible by processual archaeology, which posed a challenge to the conventional descriptive method.

Timeline of Ancient Egypt

Predynastic Period (5000–3050 BCE)
Early Dynastic Period (3050–2663 BCE)
Old Kingdom (2663–2160 BCE)
First Intermediate Period (2160–2066 BCE)
Middle Kingdom Period (2066–1650 BCE)
Second Intermediate Period (1650–1549 BCE)
New Kingdom (1549–1069 BCE)
Third Intermediate Period (1069–664 BCE)
Late Period (664–332 BCE)
Greco-Roman Period (332-30 BCE)
Roman Period (30 BCE–395 CE)
Byzantine Period (395–640 CE)
The Arabic Conquest of Egypt (642 CE)
The Ummayad Period (656–750 CE)
The Abbasid Period I and II (750–1258 CE)[2]
The Tulunids (868–905 CE)
The Ikhshidids (935–969 CE)
The Fatimids (969–1171 CE)
The Ayoubids (1171–1250 CE)
The Mamluks (1250–1517 CE)
The Ottomans (1517–1952 CE)
The French Campaign in Egypt (1798–1801 CE)

---

2. Including brief losses of power to other dynasties.

Mehmet Ali's Reign (1805–1848 CE)
Abbas Helmy I (1848–1854 CE)
Mohamed Said Pasha (1854–1863 CE)
Khedive Ismail (1863–1879 CE)
Khedive Tewfik (1879–1892 CE)
Khedive Abbas Helmy II (1892–1914 CCE)
Sultan Hussein Kamal (1914–1917 CE)
King Fuad I (1917–1936 CE)
King Farouk I (1936–1952 CE)
Mohamed Naguib (1954–1956 CE)
Gamal Abdel Nasser (1956–1970 CE)
Mohamed Anwar El-Sadat (1970–1981 CE)
Mohamed Hosni Mubarak (1981–2011 CE)

Part I
The Difficult Heritage of Egyptology

'This is a story of innocence, of deception, and infinite grief.'
Akhenaten: The Dweller in Truth by Naguib Mahfouz

This part aims to provide a deconstructed narrative of Egyptology's history, particularly from the documents of the National Archive of Egypt. It explores the colonial agendas that shaped the discipline over the nineteenth and twentieth centuries. This allows me to give voice to previously marginalised aspects of Egyptology to better understand its development and how its history has shaped its current theory and practice.

What is Egyptology?

Although a few slightly older English occurrences are known, the word 'Egyptologist' was first mentioned in the *Oxford English Dictionary* in 1859[3].

---

3. Jason Thompson and Malek 2020

The term 'Egyptology' was first translated into Arabic by the Lebanese scholar Butrus al-Bustani in his 1869 dictionary *Qamus al-Muhit*, with 'Egyptologist' ('ālim al-maṣriyāt) coming ten years later. Yet the emergence and unlocking of Egyptology as a discipline can be pinpointed to a single act of linguistic advancement: the decoding of the Rosetta Stone by a French philologist named Jean-François Champollion in 1822.[4][5]

The Ancient Egyptian language was written in various different scripts: hieroglyphic, hieratic, demotic and Coptic. However, it was hieroglyphics – a pictorial writing system – that captured the imaginations of scholars. Diverse global cultures have developed unique writing systems based on their needs and cultural evolution; despite the dominance of the alphabet in the Western world, it is not necessarily the pinnacle of writing systems. The mystique surrounding Egyptian hieroglyphs meant that when the West encountered ancient Egyptian culture, it was already being seen through the lens of the exotic and

---

4. Parkinson 2005

5. There had, of course, already been attempts to decipher the Ancient Egyptian language and its hieroglyphic script, particularly by Arabic scholars, who established that the Coptic language (the liturgical language of the Coptic Church) was the final stage of the language of the Ancient Egyptians (El-Daly 2005).

mysterious – a problematic reading that continues to plague the discipline. Biblical views of ancient Egypt fuelled this perception of ancient Egyptian culture: that hieroglyphics were cryptic images rather than a proper language and a sophisticated writing system.[6]

After Champollion's successful unlocking of the Rosetta Stone, Egyptology as a discipline progressed rapidly on two fronts: the understanding of vast collections of newly readable text; and the formation of various museological collections, many of which contained objects looted directly from Egypt. Yet Egyptology was an academic discipline conceived by Europeans and for Europeans.[7] In this book, I argue that this Eurocentric inception of Egyptology with its exclusive focus on the acquisition of 'treasures' for museums has kept it trapped in the ivory towers of Western scholarship, resulting in precious little engagement with modern and contemporary Egypt.

Egyptology is used to study ancient Egyptian civilisation across an enormous timespan: from the formation of the first cultures, to predynastic times

6. Parkinson 2005, 14–15
7. Langer, Woons and Weier 2017

before the ancient Egyptian state was formed, until
the late Roman period. It incorporates the study of
ancient Egyptian archaeology, history, anthropology,
linguistics, art history and philology. As John Baines,
Professor Emeritus of Egyptology at Oxford University,
has said, philology and archaeology complement each
other's understanding of the different ancient texts;
post-Rosetta, it was as if Egyptologists could read such
ancient texts over the shoulders of the dead.[8] Today,
Egyptology's primary purpose is to interpret such a
distant culture for the contemporary public through
mainly modern and post-modern imaginations of
ancient Egypt. As a result, Egyptologists have imposed
a chronological structure on ancient Egypt that even
Ancient Egyptians would have found highly dubious.[9]
Egyptology tries to understand ancient Egypt through
its origins, its development, its political, social and
economic systems, religious beliefs and mythology;
and how all these created its art and architecture as
a form of material culture. It has since evolved into
the study of interactions of ancient Egyptians with
their neighbours in war, peace and trade, as well as
in the fields of mathematics, astronomy, engineering,

8. Parkinson 2005, 13
9. Thompson and Malek 2020

medicine, literature and climate change. Egyptology
has also affected modern art and architecture, where
it continues to inspire artists and architects: a good
example is the Art Deco movement of the early
twentieth century, which was influenced by ancient
Egyptian art. In architecture, the distinctive 'Egyptian
Revival' style can be seen today in many European and
American buildings, inspired in part by the discovery
of Tutankhamun in 1922 and the subsequent wave
of 'Egyptomania' which permeated the art and design
industry of the time. Egyptian nationalist movements
throughout modern history have employed ancient
Egyptian art and architectural symbols to get their
message across.

Today, Egyptology lags behind its sister discipline,
archaeology, in terms of theory and praxis; however,
modern scholars are trying to bring interdisciplinary
research into the field to transform it into a more
engaged discipline, capable of bringing greater meaning to the contemporary indigenous communities of
Egypt, and to the world in general.

Egyptology: Past, Present and Future
The ancient Greeks and Romans were fascinated by
the mysterious civilisation of ancient Egypt, and many
travellers wrote accounts of their voyages along the

Nile. However, it was only in the nineteenth century that Egyptology evolved into a pseudo-academic discipline, albeit one tainted by the economic greed for antiquities fuelled by imperialistic rivalries: who would get to house the most extensive collection of Egyptian objects in their museum?[10] By the late nineteenth and early twentieth century, Egyptology was flourishing. Egyptologists discovered archaeological sites such as the Pyramids of Giza, the Valley of the Kings, and the Temples of Karnak and Luxor. Yet indigenous Egyptology suffered during that time,[11] as all archaeological sites and museums were managed by foreigners employed under Ottoman sovereignty or British colonial occupation.

In the mid-twentieth century, Egyptology evolved again, from excavation for artefacts to be exhibited in museums to a more complete study of ancient Egyptian society and culture. A new emphasis was placed on understanding the archaeological context of excavations rather than focusing solely on the artefacts removed from the sites – thereby gaining a more comprehensive understanding of Egyptian culture and society. Two major archaeologists of that

10. Fagan 2009
11. Reid 1985

time, Erik Hornung and Jan Assmann, argued that the study of ancient Egypt should be a discipline in its own right – thus giving rise to the term 'Egyptology'.

The 1952 revolution led to several changes in the field of Egyptology. Until then, Western scholars had dominated the subject, mostly holding colonial and sometimes even racist[12] attitudes towards Egyptians and their culture. After the revolution, the Egyptian government took over management of the country's archaeological sites and museums – although Egyptology's academic and scientific production mostly remained within Western institutions. At the same time, a confident post-revolution Egypt was embarking on one of the most ambitious engineering projects the country had ever seen: the High Dam, to be built across the Nile at Aswan over ten years, flooding much of the Nubian Valley. It was an extraordinary endeavour which required an equally colossal conservation effort to prevent the loss of important archaeological sites. In conjunction with the Egyptian and Sudanese governments, UNESCO launched the International Campaign to Save the Monuments of Nubia, inviting international academic institutions to help Egypt salvage important Nubian temples such

12. Challis 2013

as Abu Simbel, Kalabsha, Philae, Amada and Wadi es-Sebua, and to document all the mudbrick structures that were flooded by the dam. This campaign was a founding block in UNESCO's mandate in Egypt, ultimately helping save the country's tangible heritage. However, the campaign's immediate focus on monuments rather than people seriously impacted what remained of Nubian culture.[13]

The High Dam was completed in 1970. In 1972, Egypt ratified the UNESCO convention – and crucially, in 1983, updated its antiquities law, prohibiting the trade in and export of antiquities from Egypt. Since the 1880s, foreign archaeological missions had been entitled to half of any findings – now, they could only take publications.

Egyptology was evolving from a field focused on material remains to one attempting to employ post-modern ideas – although some of its practitioners inevitably still romanticised the colonial past. However, studies today which focus on postcolonial Egyptology, as well as feminist and reflexive understandings of the past, signify that ground-breaking research is happening in the field.[14]

---

13. Fernea, Fernea and Rouchdy 1991
14. Cooney 2018; Joyce and Meskell 2014; Matić 2016, 2023; Lemos 2023; García 2014; Langer, Woons and Weier 2017

A Napoleonic Defeat, and Decoding the Stone

I saw the way to achieve all my dreams . . . I would found a religion, I saw myself marching on the way to Asia, mounted on an elephant, a turban on my head, and in my hand a new Koran that I would have composed to suit my needs. In my enterprises, I would have combined the experiences of the two worlds, exploiting the realm of all history for my own profit.[15]

To understand the future of Egyptology, we must first delve further into its past. By the end of the eighteenth century, Egypt had long been nominally a part of the Ottoman Empire, but it was constantly being eyed by European powers. And one man in particular had designs on the region: Napoleon.[16]

---

15. Strathern 2008, 6

16. French military interest in the country extended even further back than the Ottomans: under the Ayyubid Sultan al-Malik, Egypt purchased around 12,000 youths from Eastern Europe and the Balkans to serve as mercenaries in his army. These were called the Mamelukes, which means 'owned man' or 'slave' in Arabic. The Mamelukes were children when they came to Egypt. They grew up in the Ayyubid army to fight Louis IX and the Seventh Crusade, and became the rulers of the different Egyptian provinces (Pawly and Courcelle 2012, 3–6). Many were of Turkic non-Arab and

On 13 September 1797, the commander of Italy received a letter from Napoleon telling him that 'we must seize Egypt'[17] and asking him to meet in Paris to negotiate the project. Napoleon was known to have developed an 'Oriental complex' while studying at military college in Brienne – in short, he wanted to become the Alexander the Great of his time. But his military ambition also extended further, using his illusory victories in Egypt as a platform to attack the British in India. However, Napoleon did not have the budget for his Oriental fantasies, so he dispatched his chief of staff, Berthier, to Rome to ransack Italy, from the Vatican all the way down to Napoli, an incident known as *il cavaliere saccheggiator* in Italy[18]. The

---

non-Muslim origin and barely understood Egyptian. Yet they were influenced by the Egyptian architecture of that period and built their houses, mosques, hammams and sibyls in an Egyptian fashion. If not for the Mamelukes, Egypt would have lost the battle of Ayn Jalout in 1260 against the Mongols, and much of Egypt and perhaps even most of North Africa would not have survived (Kiffer 2019). At this time, Egypt was divided into twenty-four regions, each ruled by a Mameluke Bey who had his troops. The Mamelukes never worked in the fields as *fellahin*, but kept a strong hold over them by extracting taxes and keeping them under their yoke with minimal social, economic or cultural development. All of which meant that while Egypt regularly fought off attempts from the Bedouin and Berber tribes to raid villages and take their produce, the country lacked an established army like those of the Western powers at the time.

17. Strathern 2008, 14

18. Davis 2014, 175

resulting loot, intended for the campaign in Egypt, was equivalent to three million gold francs.[19]

Napoleon brought a campaigning army of around 40,000 soldiers to Egypt, along with the famous 'savants': a group of 167 Orientalists, artists and architects, musicians and actors, biologists, medical doctors, cartographers and engineers, as well as their assistants and administrators. The troops arrived at Pompey's pillar in Alexandria at around 6 a.m. on 1 July 1798.[20] Alexandria, once a city rivalled only by Rome with its famous library, temples, palaces and monuments, had now been reduced to around 24,000 inhabitants, defended by a few fortresses built by the Mamelukes and Ottomans. Once ashore, Napoleon's army searched Alexandria for water to quench their thirst, having been reduced to drinking seawater on their voyage. In doing so, one of Napoleon's commanders, Dolomieu, explored the mosque of Attarin, converted from the ancient church of St Athanasius. Holy places were often converted for use by different faiths and the material at the site reused, and upon finding a part of the ablution fountain[21] which used a recycled seven-ton

19. Strathern 2008, 22
20. Djabarti and Moreh 1975
21. Chugg 2002

sarcophagus, Dolomieu immediately claimed it belonged to Alexander the Great.[22] The battle for Alexandria was fierce, and Mohamed Korayem, a local leader, fought bravely alongside the Mamelukes against the French. Napoleon himself declared his admiration for Korayem's courage, despite later ordering his execution in Cairo for resisting the French occupation.[23]

The route of Napoleon's campaign from Alexandria to Cairo was fraught with difficulty for the French. Villagers would gather in resistance, refusing to let the army buy food. The invading military retaliated, stealing livestock and produce and killing around nine hundred men, women and children in the process.[24] The frightful sound of men and women grieving their dead was heard for miles around as the French cut a swathe through Egypt. One of the French soldiers in the battle of Embaba on 21 July 1798 said: 'We cut off a group of the enemy so that they had to throw themselves in the Nile where many of them drowned and those that

---

22. At that time, no one could yet read hieroglyphs, so it was only a few decades later at the British Museum that the sarcophagus was confirmed as that of Nectanbo I, who died approximately thirty years before Alexander the Great conquered Egypt.

23. Strathern 2008, 131

24. Strathern 2008, 59

we reached were bayoneted . . . This resulted in a frightful carnage. The corpses of men and horses presented a hideous spectacle'.[25]

The soldiers of the French army also sexually abused the women of Egypt, where, according to the law, Muslim women who had sexual relations with other religions were sent to die – often by being thrown in the Nile tied to weights, or by beheading. The French military authorities were well aware of this but did nothing to intervene to save the lives of the women they violated. There is evidence that this horrific practice was accepted, if not actively promoted, within the French campaign in Egypt, albeit not at the highest levels.[26] Many Egyptian men and women died at the hands of the French thanks to Napoleon's belief that 'we are now obliged to accomplish great things and accomplish them we will.' Yet unrest was growing rapidly within Napoleon's factions. The Savants Corps of the French campaign were called 'braying donkeys' by their military counterparts, and many of the officers grew to distrust and dislike their more artistic compatriots, calling out, 'Donkeys

---

25. Millet and Millet 1903, 51–2
26. Djabarti and Moreh 1975

and savants in the middle!' while on the march.[27] Soon, his ambitions would meet a more decisive blow: wary of Napoleon's progress, Nelson allied with the Ottoman government, otherwise known as the Porte, to create a combined British–Ottoman army which destroyed Napoleon's fleet in the Battle of the Nile.

Stranded in Egypt with both his imperialistic delusions and a depleted army, Napoleon decided to create the *Institut d'Egypte* in Cairo to save face. The Institute's proclaimed objectives were: '1. Progress and the propagation of enlightenment in Egypt; 2. Research, study and publication of natural, industrial and historical facts concerning Egypt; 3. To advise on the different questions on which the government will consult its members.'[28] And so, the colonial birth of Egyptology was in fact a desperate piece of spin by Napoleon, partially masking a brutal military defeat. In Napoleon's Orientalist fantasies, he had instead won a 'cultural victory' via a new-found understanding of the *terra incognita* of Egypt – gaining knowledge of a past that he had previously read about only in the Bible, and the few available

---

27. Jach 2007, 16
28. *Courrier de l'Égypte*, No. 1, page 3

accounts from intrepid early travellers. To cement his reputation as a serious scholar rather than a defeated warlord, a nine-volume work known to the world as the *Description de l'Egypte*[29] was created by the savants under the orders of Napoleon himself.

ı ﻭ ﻭ ▶ ▶ ▶

On 19 July 1799, the Institut d'Egypte discussed a report sent by the mathematician-savant Lancret on the discovery of a black basalt stone near the shore of the western branch of the Nile, Rashid – also known as 'Rosetta'. The officer in charge of the discovery was Lieutenant Bouchard, who immediately recognised its importance. Lancret explained in his report that the stone bore three horizontal bands of inscriptions. The first was composed of lines written in Greek characters and possibly referred to the reign of Ptolemy Philopater; the second was of unknown characters; and the third, demotic. The stone measured about 120 cm and weighed 762 kg.[30] Lancret managed to understand the Greek inscription, discovering it to be a decree issued by the temple priests in Memphis on 27 March, 196 BCE.

---

29. Napoleon I et al. 1809
30. Parkinson 2005, 19

This extraordinary find later became known simply as the Rosetta Stone. The Institute's staff created various facsimiles of the stone so European scholars could try to work on its decipherment, but such efforts proved futile for the second section of the stone's inscription, written in the Ancient Egyptian language – a puzzle which remained unsolved until some twenty years later. During this time, ancient Egyptian objects, mummies and human remains, Coptic and Islamic manuscripts were constantly looted by the dwindling French campaign and hoarded by the Institut d'Egypte under the pretext of scholarly investigation.

Ultimately, Napoleon deserted his 'Army of the Orient in Egypt' – a decision that should have seen him court-martialled. The campaign was left first under the command of one General Minou, who had converted to Islam and married an Egyptian woman, Zobaida, in a failed attempt to blend in with the local population.[31] Minou, seeing that the tide was further turning against the French occupation,

31. Later, on 14 June 1800, during the Revolt of Cairo, Napoleon's second General, Kléber, was murdered by the Syrian scholar El-Halaby, whose dagger is exhibited at the Carcassonne Museum of Fine Arts. El-Halaby was impaled and remained on the spike until vultures devoured his corpse (Djabarti and Moreh 1975).

became increasingly attached to the Rosetta Stone: it became his private property,[32] and he hid it under his bed for safekeeping. Despite many attempts to cling to power, the French army eventually signed the treaty of Abouqir, meaning they officially had to withdraw their remaining 13,000 soldiers and savants from Egypt. The treaty also entailed that the French army return on a British ship captured in battle, along with seventeen large ancient Egyptian objects – including the Rosetta Stone – to the British and Ottoman Combined Army. These artefacts – the spoils of war, handed over as part of a military bargain – ended up in the British Museum, where they are still exhibited today.

Twenty years after the discovery and subsequent handover of the Rosetta Stone, Jean-François Champollion – ironically an ardent Bonapartist – was studying Arabic Coptic under the guidance of a Greek monk named Dom Rufail de Monakhis; a Coptic priest who had come to France from Egypt along with Napoleon's expelled army; and with Yuhanna Chiftichi, another Coptic priest who lived in Paris. It was Champollion who would make the key breakthrough. Around midday on

---

32. Letters of the Officers of the French Army, 1801

14 September 1822, he rushed to his brother's office at the Académie des Inscriptions et Belles-Lettres and upon his arrival shouted, '*Je tiens mon affaire!*' ('I have found it!') – then promptly fainted for five days.[33] The mystery of the hieroglyphics was finally solved, but the Western appetite for Egyptian treasure was stronger than ever.

Mehmet Ali, Western Consuls and the 'Rape of the Nile'

Among Nelson's combined British–Ottoman army sent in 1798 to repel Napoleon was a young commander named Mehmet Ali, who caught the attention of his superiors for his courage, shrewdness, leadership and administrative skills. Yet few could have predicted his rise to power in Egypt. Mehmet Ali was born into a humble family of tobacco traders in Kavala, in modern Greece. He gained control of Egypt during the political vacuum that took hold of the country once the French had left: in 1805, he was appointed *wali*, or governor, of the country, granting him autonomy by the Ottoman sultan to govern the region.[34] Ali worked

33. Parkinson 2005, 35
34. Fahmy 2012, 14–15

ruthlessly to consolidate his power in both the political and military realms – through economic reform, and by killing the remaining Mamelukes in the famous 'massacre of the citadel'. His notable development of Egypt's agriculture, economy and industry helped him build the first strong army to become independent from the Sultan in Istanbul, establishing military dominance and making expansionist plans in the region. He trained the *fellahin* to become soldiers under the direction of his son Ibrahim Pasha, having failed to bring enough mercenaries from Nubia and Sennar.[35]

On Pasha's visits to Egypt and Nubia, his doctor Alessandro Ricci from Siena would use his spare time to sketch the abundant antiquities in the various areas of the country, either working for himself or being commissioned by the British consul Henry Salt.[36] Using his instinctive opportunism, a now increasingly isolated Mehmet Ali saw how Salt and other consuls at the time were making a fortune as antiquities dealers. Instead of lamenting this trade, he attempted to exploit it further, all the while seeking European support for his nascent conflict

---

35. Fahmy 2002, 65–92
36. Ricci and Salvoldi 2018

with the Ottoman Sultan. Salt, along with another consul, Bernardino Drovetti, and Jean-François Champollion, fresh from his decoding of the Rosetta Stone, were permitted what was effectively a looting spree in Egypt, under the guise of concern about the 'rapid destruction of the ancient monuments'. This French–Tuscan delegation to Egypt in 1828 was met with the blessings of Mehmet Ali, who gave them *carte blanche* to take away any objects they wanted for museums back home. Champollion and Rosellini, when visiting the tomb of Seti I, hacked away two of the site's most beautiful sections instead of preserving them.

Then came a crucial intervention that shaped the entire direction of Egyptian historical preservation. Youssef Diaa Effendi and Sheikh Rifa'a al-Tahtawi (1801–73) finally convinced Mehmet Ali to issue a decree protecting Egyptian heritage.[37] In 1835, the *Wali* issued the decree for an antiquities service to be established, and a museum to be opened, in the al-Ezbekiya quarter of Cairo. Youssef Diaa Effendi was to be responsible for both under the supervision of Rifa'a al-Tahtawi, a prominent figure in Egypt during the nineteenth century who would play a

---

37. Noury 2018, 39–40

key role in the country's intellectual awakening and reform, known as 'Nahda'.

The Rise of Scientific Egyptology

Auguste Mariette arrived in Egypt in 1850, commissioned by the Louvre Museum to buy Coptic manuscripts. By the time of his arrival, the Coptic Patriarch, Pope Botros VII el-Gawli of Alexandria, had issued a decree to bring all manuscripts from the churches and monasteries to Cairo for safekeeping in the cathedral in Ezbekiyah after many had been looted or sold to antiquities dealers. Pope Botros rejected Mariette's repeated requests to buy manuscripts; Mariette, having failed in his initial assignment, spent the following year doing irreparable damage to Egyptian heritage. He exhausted the budget of 7,000 francs given to him by the Louvre to carry out illegal excavations in Saqqara, digging there hoping to find the Serapeum[38] with no *firman*. Khedive Abbas Helmy I was angry at his attempts to secure the site after discovering that a substantial trench had destroyed several

---

38. The Serapeum was associated with the worship of the Apis bull, a sacred animal the ancient Egyptians saw as an incarnation of the god Ptah.

historical layers. Mariette, like modern-day looters,[39] used to hide his loot on site, covering it with
chaff until it could be shipped in secret to France. He
returned home with no manuscripts but with large
quantities of objects illegally smuggled out of Egypt,
infuriating the Khedive. When Abbas Helmy I died,
Mariette returned to Egypt and, using diplomatic
channels, tried to convince Khedive Said to pardon
his previous crimes.[40] Through diplomatic pressure,
he convinced the Khedive Said in 1858 to appoint
him as director of the Antiquities Service.

Mariette was given unprecedented authority
over Egyptian antiquities and the Egyptian *corvée*
– a system of obligatory labour imposed by the
Ottomans on the Egyptian *fellahin*, also used for
digging the Suez Canal. During the reign of Khedive
Ismail, Heinrich Brugsch, a German Egyptologist,
convinced the Khedive to start a school to teach
Egyptians the language of their ancestors. Out of
this sadly short-lived school came Ahmed Kamal
Pasha, the first Egyptian Egyptologist to graduate
and work in the Antiquities Service. Students of
Brugsch were forbidden to study at the Egyptian

---

39. Hanna 2015, 2013
40. DWQ Dār al-Wathāʾiq al-Qawmiyya Mahafez al-Abhath

Museum of Boulaq under Mariette's orders for fear that they would learn the language of their ancestors and eventually gain agency in understanding their past.[41] Ahmed Kamal later suffered discrimination while working at the Antiquities Service, where he was prevented from taking managerial or leadership positions in favour of foreign nationals.[42]

Mariette not only clashed with Egyptians wanting to study their heritage, but also fell foul of the reforming minister of education, Ali Mubarak Pasha, who was famous for his monumental work in reforming the city of Cairo.[43] Rifa'a al-Tahtawi too struggled with Mariette and the rift grew between Egyptians, keen to reconstitute the agency to produce knowledge about their past, and the cultural colonial powers, intent on maintaining their privileged imperialist heritage. However, at the end of his tenure, Mariette realised the damage official and illegal excavations alike were doing to the archaeological sites and started regulating the objects leaving Egypt. Mariette fell out of favour with the Khedive when he was prevented from

41. Reid 1985, 233–246
42. DWQ Dār al-Wathā'iq al-Qawmiyya Nizārat al-Ashghāl al-'Āmma (Ministry of Public Works)-b
43. Fahmy 2018, 109–144

giving Queen Ahhotep's jewellery to Queen Eugenie
of France, who visited Egypt to inaugurate the Suez
Canal.

Layered Colonialism

Due to the wasteful overspending of Khedive Ismail,
Egypt found itself under the yoke of Western bankers
– a situation that worsened after Egypt was pushed
to sell shares in the Suez Canal Company to Britain in
1875 for much less than they were worth. Egyptians
were deemed unfit to manage their finances, and
several Western institutions were established in
the country to monitor their financial affairs and
ensure that their debtors were paid. Khedive Ismail
was deposed in favour of his son Tewfik, who was
more compliant with the British, but could not stop
a revolt to free Egypt from Western control. The
British and the French, who owed money to Egypt,
sent warships, further angering the Egyptians:
anti-European protests broke out, leaving more than
two thousand Egyptians dead. The British, growing
tired with the situation, declared war, bombarding
Alexandria heavily from the sea until they gained a
decisive win on 13 September 1882, in the battle at
Tell el-Kebir. It was the beginning of an occupation
that would last for around seventy years. The first

person to restore order was the Marquis of Dufferin and Ava, who had Egyptological interests and had excavated at Deir el-Bahari in 1859. Dufferin had a huge collection of antiquities he had unearthed or bought from Egypt. Lord Francis Grenfell, who became Egyptian Sirdar for three years, excavated in Aswan, purchased a massive collection from the antiquities market, and served on the Antiquities Service Committee.

Lord Cromer, who replaced Dufferin in 1892, expressed his dislike of antiquities, saying, 'I wish there was [sic] no antiquities in this country; they are more trouble than anything else'.[44] Later, both Cromer and Grenfell served as president of the Egypt Exploration Fund, established by Amelia Edwards in 1882 and dedicated to studying ancient Egyptian material from a biblical perspective; they excavated in Tell al-Maskhuta in the Delta to create a narrative for the biblical Exodus. Cromer transferred the Antiquities Service from the Khedival court to the Ministry of Public Works, although its management remained under the French. In 1881, Gaston Maspero had taken over the direction of the department from Auguste Mariette (he remained

---

44. Sayce 1923, 72

until 1886) despite the more qualified man for the position being Heinrich Brugsch. It was now the British and not the Khedive who appointed government officials.

The feud between the French and the British monopoly over Egyptian heritage, which had continued since the battle of Abouqir in 1799, was reignited after an encounter at Fashoda in southern Sudan when the French and British military units almost joined battle again. The French, a century later, still resented the loss of their colonial influence over Egypt; as one French journalist wrote, 'If modern Egypt has escaped our influence, largely by our own fault, ancient Egypt remains and will remain French'.[45]

In 1892 Eugène Grébaut became Maspero's successor as head of the Antiquities Service. Despite his experience in Egypt and his knowledge of Arabic and Egyptology, Grébaut's reign as director-general was marred by inefficiency, blatant favouritism towards the French, and carelessness regarding archaeological concessions.[46] Despite his dislike of antiquities dealers, he became one himself, opening

45. Gady 2005, 609
46. Jason Thompson 2015b, 25–28

a museum sales room which continued to operate for nearly a century. The Frenchman proposed as his replacement was Albert Daninos, a former assistant to Auguste Mariette and highly experienced in the Antiquities Service, having discovered the famous statues of Rahotep and Nofret from Meidum, currently in the Egyptian Museum.[47] Although Daninos was French, had trained in the Louvre and knew the Antiquities Service inside out, Xavier Charmes, a high-ranking official at the French Ministry of Public Instruction, and the French consul general revoked his candidacy. They both said that they could not guarantee that he would protect French interests in Egyptology because of his Algerian origins, and that his loyalties would be under question.[48] Daninos had further problems: he was Jewish at a time when anti-Semitic sentiments were brewing in France after Captain Alfred Dreyfus of the French army gave important secret documents to the Imperial German military. Such sentiments that the French had a monopoly over the Antiquities Service are also echoed in this letter to the prime minister of Egypt, Ahmed Kamal Pacha, in

---

47. Bruwier 1989
48. Jason Thompson 2015b, 63

1894 when Daninos protested at how he was continuously being bypassed in the service in favour of
French officials:

> The Antiquities Service has a French director and
> Prussian deputy and two assistants to the deputy
> director. I have been informed that the deputy director,
> Brugsch Bey, will resign now or after he returns from
> his leave. In addition, I have been told that the dir-
> ector had agreed with him to render this resignation
> in secret, so I do not know about it. He goes ahead
> and appoints a French person from abroad. Using
> the pretext that this person has extra knowledge. As
> is the custom in similar matters. Alternatively, they
> suggested appointing Darcey instead of Brugsch
> even though I am more qualified for him for the
> following reasons: Firstly, I am more senior than him
> because I have been in service for twenty-one years
> while he has been in service for six. We are at the
> same administrative level, and our academic know-
> ledge is the same. In addition to my exceeding him
> because I know Arabic. Secondly, he does not have a
> degree that I lack. Thirdly, his father is an antiquities
> dealer in France, so it is wrong to appoint him as a
> deputy director for that specific reason. Fourthly, the
> museum is a national museum, and Egypt is deprived

of knowing the science of antiquities. Appointing me in this position does not harm the interests of France or England, given that no French person or English person has been harmed since the establishment of the Antiquities Service until now. I remain your humble servant.[49]

When Maspero returned as head of the Antiquities Service for another term (1899–1914), he came under further pressure by Lord Cromer to appoint Britons to senior posts in the Antiquities Service and the museums. The British already did most of the archaeological fieldwork in Egypt; now Cromer also wanted to see them in the administration. The French resisted; however, James Quibell and Howard Carter were appointed to the service after negotiating with the British. During this period, Maspero shifted the central budget of the Antiquities service from excavation towards restoration works at the various sites.[50]

Ahmed Kamal had studied in Madrassat al-Lissan al-Qadim, the first school of ancient language started under Ali Mubarak's initiative in 1869. It was the

49. DWQ Dār al-Wathāʾiq al-Qawmiyya Nizārat al-Ashghāl al-ʿĀmma (Ministry of Public Works)-b
50. David 1999, 208

first school of Egyptology funded by Ismail Pasha
and was headed by Heinrich Brugsch. Several of its
students studied Egyptian, English, French, German,
Coptic and Amharic.[51] Fearing that they would eventually take the role of the French in the Antiquities
Service, Auguste Mariette did his best to stop the
students' academic progress;[52] Kamal was the first
Egyptian who truly broke the Western barriers
of Egyptology, even if only to the extent that was
allowed for him. His frustrations, though seldom
expressed, showed how he was forbidden from
taking any actual managerial position within the
Antiquities Service despite having vast experience in
excavation. He was the archaeologist who cleared
the Deir el-Bahari Cache (Theban Tomb 320, or the
Royal Cache, where the priests of the twenty-first
Dynasty hid royal mummies to protect them from
theft), discovered by the Sheikh Ali Abd Al-Rassoul
family today as Theban Tomb 320.[53] He was usually
bypassed for promotion in favour of much less
qualified French or British personnel; despite such
discouragements, he published many vital reports
and articles in the Annales du Service des Antiquités.

---

51. DWQ Dār al-Wathā'iq al-Qawmiyya Diwan al-Madares
52. Reid 1985, 235
53. Wilson 1964, 84

His lifetime project was a monumental dictionary of Ancient Egyptian language, which failed to see the light for lack of support from the French and British Egyptologists. Today, his grandchildren have given his archival notes for the dictionary to the Bibliotheca Alexandrina; perhaps his project will bear fruit in a few years.

A few years before he died, Kamal asked Pierre Lacau, the head of the Antiquities Service after Maspero, to include more Egyptians in the service, but his requests fell on deaf ears. 'Lacau dismissed the notion as unworthy of consideration. Except for Kamal and Ahmed Najib, another student of the school of al-Lissan al-Qadim, he declared no Egyptians had shown any interest in the antiquities of their country.'

'M. Lacau,' Kamal responded, 'in the sixty-five years you French have directed the Service, what opportunities have you given us?'[54]

Who is the Looter?

Since the beginning of the history of Egyptology, there had been antagonism against the inhabitants of Sheikh Abd al-Qurna in Luxor, particularly the

54. Wilson 1964, 192–193

family of Sheikh Abd al-Rassul, who discovered the
Deir el-Bahari Cache. The historical accounts suggest
that the Qurnawi understood excavations and the
antiquities trade well; many so-called archaeologists
or antiquities dealers found competition there.[55] The
residents of al-Qurna made a meagre income after
the French expedition to Egypt by selling antikas[56] in
the 1820s and 30s. When Mehmet Ali's consuls went
round Egypt to pillage objects they could sell to
museums in Europe, they made excellent use of the
Qurnawi, who according to Giovanni d'Athanasi,
the antiquities collector who worked at the service
of Henry Salt, the British Consul in Egypt at the
time of Mehmet Ali, were 'very ready and useful at
such work; they understand antiquities as well as a
European antiquary, and whenever they find a rare
morsel of antiquity, recollecting that a similar piece
had never been found in the course of excavations,
they ask no trifling price for it from anyone who
may want to have it.'[57] Egyptologists who themselves caused irreparable damage to Egyptian
archaeological sites – such as Edouard Naville,
whose excavations in Deir el-Bahari destroyed a huge

---

55. Van der Spek 2011; Tully and Hanna 2013; Colla 2008
56. Van Der Spek 2008
57. D'Athanasi 1836, 135

Coptic monastery without documentation – nevertheless looked down on the Qurnawi, condemning
them as robbers, looters and treasure hunters.[58] It
was acceptable for European antiquities traders and
excavators to make huge profits from the collections
sold to museums or private collectors; yet locals sub-
sisting on such activities were vilified for over two
hundred years of Egyptology until they were forcibly
relocated at the beginning of the twenty-first century.

Gaston Maspero rarely permitted Egyptians to
excavate, usually saying he would not do so because
Egyptians were fuelled only by a desire to find
treasures rather than by a spirit of scientific inquiry.[59]
When it was time for Lord Cromer to leave power, he
informed his successor, Sir Edon Gorst, in 1904 that
Egyptians were not 'nearly civilised enough to care
about the preservation of their ancient monuments'.[60]
Further evidence of the alienation of Egyptians and
their exclusion from scholarship can be witnessed
on the façade of the Egyptian Museum in Cairo
in Tahrir Square, designed by Marcel Dourgnon
in 1901. The façade celebrates the forefathers of
Egyptian Egyptology without mentioning a single

58. Van der Spek 2011
59. Jason Thompson 2015b, 188
60. Welch 1988, 285

Egyptian: Rifa'a al-Tahtawi, Ali Mubarak (1823–93) and even Joseph Hekekyan Bey, who excavated in Memphis and Heliopolis, are all absent. No Egyptian was regarded as worth mentioning on the façade; even Horapollo, probably an Egyptian who wrote Hieroglyphica, which is an explanation of the signs in Greek, was mentioned in the 'Res Aegyptiacas Conscripserunt'.[61] Such obliteration of any Egyptian role in their study was not coincidental but had been intentional since the French campaign in Egypt.

The 1912 Law

Under the reign of Abbas Helmy II, who had a strained relationship with the country's British colonial administration,[62] Egypt passed the '1912 law' based on the Khedival decree of 1891. Even though the law favoured citizens with diplomatic privileges, these highly unequal rules sentenced Egyptians guilty of illegal excavation to a year in prison and a fine of ten Egyptian pounds – an enormous sum for an Egyptian – while a European guilty of the same offence was sentenced to at most a week in prison and a fine of one Egyptian

---

61. Reid 2003, 3–4
62. Sayyid-Marsot 1969

pound. Law enforcement regarding the division of finds between 1891 and 1912 had been feeble, and Maspero was often lenient towards European missions. He colluded against Egypt's interests because he thought finds – including portraits now in the collection at the Petrie Museum – would be better preserved in London than in Cairo thanks to the limited storage and display facilities for which he was responsible.[63] International bodies were permitted to fund and conduct excavations under Maspero's loose supervision since they did not cost him anything. Such laxity led to the loss of Nefertiti's bust in the division of the finds by the Antiquities Service with Borchardt.[64] Maspero also encouraged museums and collectors to buy antiquities through the Antiquities Service;[65] the provenance of such acquisitions was so loose that Arthur Weigal called them 'stray cats and dogs.'[66]

When the 1912 law was passed shortly before World War I, Egypt received hysterical protests from many Western working institutions. The British Academy wrote to the Egyptian government:

---

63. Jason Thompson 2015b, 123
64. Hanna 2023
65. Jason Thompson 2015b, 123
66. Jason Thompson 2015b, 126–127

In the case of Greece and Italy, the intimate dependence of modern civilisation on that of the Greeks and Romans will always ensure support of excavation, despite complete restriction of exports; but Egypt is not in the same position, and interest must be kept alive by showing to foreigners the portable works of sculptures and painting and minor arts that she produced in antiquity.[67]

The council of the British Association for the Advancement of Science protested:

Since these foreign investigations are supported almost entirely by voluntary contribution from persons interested in providing proper equipment for the scientific study of Egyptology in their own countries, there is grave reason to fear that if the objects recovered by these expeditions are wholly or for the most part retained in Egypt, on whatever plea of scientific or other necessity these contributions will be diverted to other branches of learning, and to other countries where the policy of the governments is more in accord with the general

67. DWQ (Dār al-Wathā'iq al-Qawmiyya Nizārat al-Ashghāl al-'Āmma (Ministry of Public Works)-a

interests of learning and education . . . The result, if foreign contributions are withheld, must be that a large body of native labour will be thrown out of remunerative employment annually and that the present annual influx of visitors, which is greatly stimulated both by the spectacle of excavations in progress and by the display of newly discovered material for study on museums abroad, will be diverted elsewhere.[68]

The same colonialist narrative was echoed in the Royal Asiatic Society: 'Moreover, the Egyptian peasant will be deprived of both direct and indirect benefits. Not only will the large wages for diggings annually paid to a considerable body of the peasant folk cease entirely, but local business will diminish in the ratio of the reduction of tourists.'[69]

Independence Attempts at the Feet of the Boy King

Lord Carnarvon was a British nobleman whose wife had a considerable inheritance. The couple led a typical British aristocratic life, and Lord Carnarvon

68. ibid.
69. ibid.

came to Egypt during his recovery from a motor-sport accident, having been advised by Lady Cromer to take up Egyptology to improve his morale. Maspero encouraged Carnarvon for financial reasons, and in 1905 he was awarded his first concession in the north of Assasif, then in Dra Abou el-Naga in Theban Tomb 15, belonging to Tetiky. He found the famous stela of Kamose – known as the Carnarvon Stela – in 1908. Yet Carnarvon was careless in handling the excavations; Arthur Weigall wrote of him as being entirely irresponsible.[70] Carnarvon, like many of his peers, described the Egyptian men working on his dig as 'a willing and hard-working lot', later elaborating that they were 'no more dishonest than other Egyptian *fellahin*'.[71] Such demeaning and racist comments have always been part of Egyptology and shaped the 'daily interactions and academic thinking of "Western" scholars . . . Racism inherent in Egyptology; a racism that was, in fact, its reason of existence'.[72]

Carnarvon, aware of his shortcomings, asked Maspero to recommend someone to handle his excavations; Maspero gladly suggested Howard Carter,

---

70. Jason Thompson 2015b, 138
71. Carnarvon, Carter, and Griffith 1912, 1
72. Riggs 2021, 67

who had been forced to resign from the Antiquities
Service due to an incident with some drunk French
tourists, whom he had asked the Egyptian custodians
of Saqqara to forbid from vandalising the site. After
leaving the Antiquities Service, Carter spent several
years working as an artist and an antiquities dealer,
making much less money and commanding far less
prestige than before. He immediately accepted work
back in excavation. First, he helped Carnarvon
finalise his excavations in Theban Tomb 15, before
moving on to other sites, from which Carnarvon
expected to find worthwhile antiquities he could sell
to fund his excavations.[73] The two men had no idea
of the fame they were about to acquire.

Carter took a house on Elwet el-Dibban in the
Theban Necropolis, known today as Carter House.
Carnarvon, despite making steady progress, wanted
a sensational discovery to justify his increasing
number of excavations work permits. After much
debate, Maspero before his retirement awarded
Carnarvon a concession in the Valley of the Kings,
previously thought to have been completely cleared
out. Using his skill as an Egyptologist, Carter deduced
that although that the Valley of the Kings had been

73. Goode 2007, 76

cleared, it had never been *systematically* worked
over. And he had one particular prize in mind. He
wrote, 'We had definite hopes of finding the tomb of
one particular king, and that King Tutankhamun'.[74]
However, the concession contract entailed that no
undiscovered tombs would be subject to division or
removal. This was a blow to Carter, who continued
to trade heavily in antiquities and would do so for
the rest of his life, working behind a third party to
bypass scrutiny.[75]

After the war's end, Carter resumed excavations
in the Valley of the Kings. While he was cleaning
a section near the tomb of Ramesses VI, his *Rais*
(expedition leader), Ahmed Gergar, found a series
of steps; it was clear that this was an entrance to
a possibly untouched tomb. Carter dispatched a
telegram to Carnarvon, who arrived at speed so that
they could open the tomb together. On 26 November
1922, Carter opened the tomb, and when Carnarvon
asked what he saw, he responded with the famous
'Wonderful things.'[76] The documentation and clearing of the tomb took some time; Carter asked for
the help of the Metropolitan Museum mission to

74. Carter and Mace 2014, 122
75. Jason Thompson 2018, 44
76. James 2006

manage the flow of tourists already flocking to the site. Carnarvon, meanwhile, had given exclusive rights to *The Times* newspaper to discuss the discovery's development.

Yet both Carnarvon and Carter were entirely tone-deaf to the political developments in Egypt after the 1919 revolution and the declaration of independence from British occupation on 28 February 1922. Their handling of the Tutankhamun site caused fierce political battles between the Egyptian government, headed by Marcus Hanna Pasha, the Minister of Public Works; and the Antiquities Service, led by Pierre Lacau, Carter and Carnarvon. As a result, Carnarvon was forced to rescind his lucrative agreement with *The Times*, leaving the world's media free to cover the story. The Egyptian press was particularly excited about the discovery; reporters from the country's newspapers flocked to the tomb, only to be faced with a visibly annoyed Carter.[77] He had misjudged how important the 'discovery of the century' was for Egypt following its independence: it was a cultural means for the political leadership, the elite, and the various social classes to find a newfound pride in their past – a pride that reflected the new

---

77. Colla 2008, 192

political shifts they were going through. Carter, however, retained his colonial convictions, quarrelling with the French director of the Antiquities Service and the Egyptian inspectors hired to supervise his work. After taking his time to clear and adequately photograph the tomb, an uneasy solution was found; Egypt would keep all the objects in the tomb and pay the heir, Lord Carnarvon, all his expenses.[78] Yet even this astonishing find was not enough for Carter: he secretly pocketed a few objects from the tomb, which King Faruq later managed to restore in confidence.[79] And, as a final insult to the Egyptians, Carter removed the excavation notes (today kept at the Griffith Institute in Oxford), stripping away locals' agency to produce any knowledge about the collection or its objects.

Tutankhamun's discovery changed everything: the world's views on archaeology, Egyptology, and the past itself; breathless rumours of a curse only intensified curiosity around 'King Tut'. The country would even use this burgeoning 'Egyptomania' as 'soft power' in later years. The gold mask of the young king, and his fantastic jewellery, were emblems

---

78. DWQ Dār al-Wathā''iq al-Qawmiyya (The Foreign Affairs) al-Khargiyya
79. Goode 2007, 91

of the Egyptian past that shaped the world's image of Egypt.[80]

A Pause Between the Two Wars

The period between the two world wars was characterised by the rise of national movements in the Middle East, directly affecting archaeological practice in the region. Europe was suffering the financial ramifications of World War I, because of which the Americans were better able to fund excavations in Egypt. Americans coming to the Middle East still carried the notions of religious and racial superiority endemic to the West at that time, writing from their ivory towers about indigenous populations as the 'natives'.[81] Archaeologists who retained what were later called Orientalist ideologies were detested by local intellectuals who witnessed their detachment both from the present and from other historical periods of Egypt such as the medieval or Islamic. Such archaeologists were often characterised by their biblical leanings and a refusal to engage with Islam and the Arab world. They rarely paid attention to the meanings to the local

---

80. Riggs 2021
81. Goode 2007, 9

people of the sites and objects they found. At that time, the rhetoric of 'world heritage' had its roots: that such objects did not belong to the people of the nations being colonised. Instead, they belonged to all of humanity, regardless of where they were found. Such attitudes were typified by one of the pioneers of American Egyptology, James Henry Breasted, America's first formally trained Egyptologist[82], who in a letter to his wife said, 'God save Egypt from the Egyptians'.[83]

With American influence growing in the inter-war period, Breasted thought that a total monopoly on ancient Egypt could be achieved by building a new museum and research institute funded by the Rockefellers, but since he proved tone-deaf to what Egyptian intellects and nationalists were discussing in terms of managing their past, permission for the project was refused.[84] Breasted had also expressed several times how detrimental it would be to Western Egyptology if Egyptians themselves were allowed to study abroad, antagonising any that did, and writing letters opposing their employment at the Antiquities

---

82. Abt 2012
83. Goode 2007, 76
84. DWQ Dār al-Wathā'iq al-Qawmiyya al-Khārgiyya (The Foreign Affairs)

Service.[85] Breasted wanted the Rockefellers to fund a museum and an institute to teach Egyptology away from 'nationalist' narratives. Herbert Winlock, another American head of the Metropolitan Museum of Art's Egyptian Expedition, expressed his disdain for Egyptians as 'intellectually oblique' and incapable of understanding the great works of archaeology.[86]

The conspiracy against Egyptian Egyptology was not exclusively American, but most Western Egyptologists preferred a French or British appointment to that of an Egyptian for fear that such a transition would eliminate all of them. Even King Fuad, a monarch of Turkish origin, supported Étienne Drioton as successor to Pierre Lacau rather than Selim Hassan, despite indigenous calls for the head of the service to be an Egyptian.

'He Usurped my Moment of Glory'

Another pioneer of Egyptian Egyptology at that time was Labib Habachi (1906–84), a student of the most prominent philosophical thinker and reformer of the Egyptian educational system, Taha Hussein (1889–1973).[87] Habachi came from a small village

85. Reid 2015, 109
86. Seton-Thompson 1923, 134
87. Ahmed 2021; Colla 2008

in Mansoura and decided to study Egyptology at
Fuad I University after first opting for mathematics,
which he found he disliked. He enjoyed studying under the Russian Vladimir Golénischeff, who
trained many Egyptians. Habachi was famous for
publications such as *The Obelisks of Egypt*, which
he published in his later years. Throughout his
career, Habachi experienced the same attitude from
the Western archaeologists he worked with: they
continually patronised him, convincing him that he
was not good enough. However, the incident that
hurt him most involved the Belgian Egyptologist
Constant de Wit. During Habachi's season in Aswan
on Elephantine Island and at the tombs of Qubbet
al-Hawa in 1946–7, he made significant discoveries
that changed the area's history. He took plenty of
time to write and publish for fear of the usual condescending criticism from his Western colleagues.
However, to his shock, he found that De Wit had
gone one step further, stealing his finds, taking
pictures and presenting them at the International
Congress of Orientalists in Paris in 1949.[88] Jill
Kamil, a biographer of Habachi, describes De Wit's
presentation of Habachi's discovery, which provides

---

88. Kamil 2007, 170–171

an explicit example of the condescending attitude of many Western scholars towards local archaeologists in the first half of the twentieth century. 'De Wit would never have treated one of his students in such a manner, let alone a Western colleague. With an Egyptian, it caused him no disquiet.'[89] 'He usurped my moment of glory,' elaborated Habachi.[90]

Superficial Nationalism

The liberal experiment that had started in 1922 ended with a military coup backed by the public, who took to the streets in 1952. This would be later identified as the July 23 revolution. For the first time since ancient Egypt, Egyptians finally ruled their country.[91] Yet this was also when the defeated European colonial powers started to regain a footing in Egyptology. The French had Christiane Desroches Noblecourt, a Louvre Museum Curator and an established Egyptologist who worked as the UNESCO advisor to the Centre des études et de documentation d'archéologie égyptienne (CEDAE), who had powerful political connections[92] and later played an

---

89. Kamil 2007, 170–171
90. Kamil 2007, 171
91. Sayyid-Marsot 2007, 126
92. Jason Thompson 2018, 228

essential role in the Nubian campaign. The English remained a notorious enemy of French control over the service, but the presence of British officials within the Antiquities Service was dying out; their replacements were Egyptians such as Mahmoud Hamza, who became the director of the Cairo Museum in 1941–50. Furthermore, British personnel who taught Egyptology at Fuad I University were also being replaced by Egyptians. However, after 23 July 1952, all Egyptologists who had spent their summer in Europe lost their positions in the Antiquities Service. The new director, Mustafa Amer, was trained at the University of Liverpool and came from the former Fuad I University, now renamed Cairo University. The transition was uneasy: there was no handover, and the situation seemed precarious for some time, but it was eventually put in order.

Despite the general rejection of the European powers, Amer knew that funding and knowledge production was still in the hands of Britain, France, Germany and the United States. He tried to restore ties with his usual diplomacy to keep excavations going. In 1958, Mohammed Zakaria Ghoneim was appointed as director of the Egyptian Museum in Cairo; however, he faced extreme antagonism due to his strong stance on curbing the illegal trade in antiquities. He was accused of illegally exporting objects from Saqqara, and on 12 January 1959 he was found drowned in the Nile; some say he committed suicide, while others say that he was framed. After his death, Jean-Philippe Lauer, who was now the leading archaeologist of Saqqara, asked for an audit of objects at the Cairo Museum, and the objects were found, proving Ghoneim's innocence after his death.[93]

'We would be treated better if we were statues'

In 1954, Gamal Abdel Nasser decided to build a High Dam seven kilometres south of the Aswan Dam, constructed during British rule under the aegis of William Wilcocks, the Minister of Public Works under Lord Cromer. The High Dam was an ambitious project but was beyond Egypt's financial capacity. Nasser first looked for funding with the Americans, who refused, then, based on the world's political chessboard at the time, asked the Soviets instead. Such ambitions were hampered by the tripartite invasion in 1956 by Britain, France and Israel after the nationalisation of the Suez Canal.[94]

93. Jason Thompson 2018, 259
94. Berque 1972

British Prime Minister Anthony Eden wanted to unseat Nasser to avenge the loss of Suez but ended up losing the war, getting toppled from office himself, and throwing salt on the Arab–Israeli conflict in the process. The conflict also halted British and French archaeological missions working in Egypt, as their permits were halted until the conflict was resolved and diplomatic ties reinstated.

The project of the High Dam continued; designed by the Soviets on an enormous scale, it is estimated that around 30,000 Egyptians and 2,000 experts from the Soviet Union worked for eight years to finish it. Nasser boastfully said, 'In antiquity, we built pyramids for the dead. Now we build new pyramids for the living'.[95] The High Dam's benefits were essential to Nasser's efforts to achieve industrial independence; however, the ramifications for Nubian heritage were devastating. Mustafa Amer, circulated a report on the salvage of the monuments of Nubia in June 1955, but the only response came from the Metropolitan Museum, not offering help but rather asking to buy one or two Nubian temples.[96] In 1958, Tharwat Okasha was appointed as Minister of Culture and

95. Fahim 2013, 14
96. D'Auria and Josephson 2010, 224–227

National Guidance; as Egypt's former military attaché to UNESCO, he contacted UNESCO and asked for help. UNESCO was still a new organisation, but it managed to rescue the monuments by finding funding for the various archaeological missions. Many missions refused to work in Nubia because they could not bring back worthwhile antiquities for their museums. The archaeological work was also criticised for its lack of accurate documentation of anything not ancient, such as artefacts from Christian and Islamic Nubia. The Nubians have suffered dramatically from such forced displacement and lack of attention from UNESCO, the archaeological missions and the Egyptian state; in the words of one Nubian, 'We would be treated better if we were statues.'[97]

As an organisation, UNESCO has based its philosophy and *modus operandi* on the Nubian Salvage campaign. Such work today is heavily criticised as having focused merely on the monuments rather than on the people, and for reinforcing the idea of 'world heritage', stripping agency from the local people to preserve, study and benefit from their heritage.[98]

---

97. R. A. Fernea and Gerster 1973; E. W. Fernea, Fernea, and Rouchdy 1991
98. Meskell 2018, 28–58

Part II
Egyptology Now

Kant said that theory without practice is empty, while practice without theory is blind. This part discusses how Egyptology as a discipline has evolved primarily through practice and much less through theory and how this has affected the history written about ancient Egypt. The chapter attempts to link practice with theory and the different schools of Egyptology, and to explore how the social sciences evolved with social theory while Egyptology has lagged behind – even as the study of archaeology itself has moved forward.

We have dealt – as we think, adequately – with the problems connected with that. Perhaps some later (scholar), aided by the divine gifts of a sound mind and of solid scholarship, will penetrate into these problems in greater detail than we did here. A person who creates a new discipline does not have the task of enumerating all the problems connected with it. His task is to specify the subject of the discipline and its various branches and the discussions connected with it. His successors, then, may gradually add more problems, until the discipline is completely [presented].[99]

Ancient Egypt was Already the Past by the New Kingdom

The ancient Egyptians believed in the notion of cyclical history. They believed that the world was recreated daily with the cycles of Nut, the sky mother goddess who ate the sun god Re at dawn to give birth to him again at dusk. This was part of their rebirth and resurrection belief system: *izfet* and *maat*, Seth and Horus. The Egyptians also experienced the idea of cyclical history: they saw kingdoms and dynasties rise, decline, then fall, and then experience reunification and further growth and flourishing. Ancient Egyptian history was part of their belief system; they imagined that after death, they would

---

rise again to the fields of *iaru* and live there. This cyclical view of the world was also apparent in their understanding of time. Time-telling in ancient Egypt had been evident since its prehistory in Nabta Playa, where the world's first sundial was discovered. Clepsydrae and other sundial designs were found in temples. The Egyptians recognised solar years and measured time astronomically with precision.[100] The ancient Egyptians kept track of time by counting the regnal years of their monarchs, which is how they dated the kings' births, achievements and wars. The ancient Egyptians commemorated their ancestors on king lists that supposedly originated when the gods ruled on earth, and that is how they connected the present to the past.

The complete king list is inscribed on the walls of the temples of Seti I and Ramesses II of the New Kingdom at Abydos in Sohag in Upper Egypt. Another essential reference is the Palermo Stone, a stela of unknown provenance that ended up in Sicily in 1877[101] and is one of several fragments found in different museums and known as the Royal Annals. Some tombs and sarcophagi also bore evidence

---

100. Neugebauer 2012
101. Wilkinson 2012, 20

of king lists dating to different periods. The most complete was found intact in 1824 by Bernardino Drovetti, one of the consuls who worked as antiquities dealers under Mehmet Ali; however, due to poor handling, by the time it arrived in Italy it was reduced to a few readable fragments written in hieratic. The lists not only put the kings in chronological order, but some also referred to their regnal years. There are many speculations as to why the ancient Egyptians created these lists, the general view being that they made them in order to establish the legitimacy of their kings' reign; however, there is no evidence that Egyptians looked at history so differently from today. Ancient Egyptians edited out the historical periods that seemed turbulent to them, such as the reigns of Akhenaten or Hatshepsut. Such a subjective view of the past showed that there could have been an 'official' accepted narrative of the past that was recorded in stone rather than a documentation of the events.

Another means by which the Egyptians used to document the past was the autobiographies inscribed in their tombs, such as the famous autobiography of Harkhuf in Sheikh Abu el-Hawa in Aswan, where he writes the fascinating story of King Pepi II and the pygmy brought from the land of Yam. Ancient

Egyptians also, as part of the cult of the dead, visited the tombs of their ancestors to restore their names, talked about them to keep their names alive, wrote prayers, and left offerings of bread and flowers.

The person considered the first Egyptologist in ancient Egypt is Prince Khaemwaset, the son of Ramesses II of the New Kingdom. Khaemwaset restored and expanded the cult of the Apis bull in Saqqara and had a particular interest in visiting the Old Kingdom monuments in the Memphite Necropolis. He restored the pyramids at Giza and the sun temples of Abusir.[102] He also carried out excavations, from which he discovered the statue of Kawab, a prince of King Khufu, while documenting his activities on the walls of such monuments and reusing blocks of the Old Kingdom for his own monument[103] – a tradition which continues in Egypt to this day. Not only were blocks reused, but in the Late Period, many designs for tombs and temples used Old Kingdom or other, older designs in an archaising trend that was fashionable at the time.

Ancient Egypt inspired the Greeks in the Late Period. One of the ancient revival styles in Egypt

102. Kawai 2013, 1–2
103. Gomaà 1973

is the Doric Order, which originated in Middle Kingdom architecture in Beni Hassan. In Homer's *Iliad*, Egyptians are mentioned as being good with medicine through their different plants, good doctors, and the 'hundred gates of Thebes'.[104] The famous Greek historian Herodotus of Halicarnassus visited Egypt in the fifth century BCE when the country was under Persian rule. His account described the geography, climate and agriculture of Egypt. He also detailed the manners and customs of the ancient Egyptians and how they differed from the rest of the world. He described gender roles quite different from those of ancient Greece and how women in ancient Egypt had a much more significant role than in the rest of the world. He said the Nile was so fertile that it alone could make Egyptian women pregnant. Herodotus also wrote about the kings of the Old Kingdom who built the Pyramids, such as Khufu, Khafre and Menkaure. He did not travel widely in Egypt, gathering its descriptions from third parties, and much of his work has come across as quite implausible.

A more important work, produced much later in antiquity, is that of Manetho in the third century BCE.

---

104. Derby 1864

Manetho was a native Egyptian living in Alexandria who spoke and wrote in Greek, the lingua franca of Alexandria and the Mediterranean. Manetho's main work, *Ægyptiaka of Hecataeus*, was not found in a complete volume, as ancient Egyptians relied on oral history to transmit knowledge.[105] Any written text by Manetho was probably lost, and what has remained is the later citations of other authors. As an Alexandrian, Manetho is criticised for seeing the world only from the perspective of Lower Egypt rather than Upper Egypt. Despite such criticism, Egyptology still adheres today to his division of ancient Egyptian history into thirty dynasties. He also offered insights into ancient Egyptian religion and culture and Egypt's interactions with neighbouring civilisations.

Ibn Khaldun and Medieval Arab Scholars

As the ancient Egyptians believed in cyclical history, Ibn Khaldun (1336–1406), a medieval philosopher of history, by observing the political situation around him, wrote his theory of cyclical history, describing it through the concept of 'Asabiyah'. Ibn Khaldun was born in Tunis and was possibly of Andalusian descent, although his name suggests his father's

---

105. Waddell 2018, 4–8

lineage was Yemeni. His work primarily built on
that of his Arabic predecessors, Ibn Sina (Avicenna)
and Ibn Rushd (Averroes), while having a critical
view of the time's metaphysical, social and religious
phenomena. Such critique made Ibn Khaldun the
most prominent figure in the social sciences between
Aristotle and Machiavelli.[106] He was one of the first
thinkers to relate to history as a present practice in
his famous epistemological work, the *Muqaddima*
or *Prolegomena*. 'The past resembles the future as
water resembles water'.[107] According to this idea,
studying the present enlightens us about the past,
and analysing the past gives us material to understand the present and the future. In the rest of his
book, he presents a sociology of knowledge, politics,
economics, and cultural and urban life. Ibn Khaldun
tried to theorise the nature of history and wrote
that all attempts to write about an objective past
are futile. He stressed the fact that each individual
author writes history according to the different
experiences he goes through.

Ibn Khaldun devised several factors that make
writing about the past in an unbiased, neutral manner

---

106. Khaldūn and Issawi 1992, 2
107. Khaldûn et al. 2020, 30

impossible. These factors range from creed, bias, opinion, partisanship and overconfidence, through failure to understand the historical source, mistaking belief for truth, inability to grasp complex historical contexts and, most important, the lack of understanding of the laws governing the transformation of human society in different historical periods.[108] He concludes that the researcher of the past needs to understand the nature of events, the changes and the conditions governing them in order to understand history. Only through accurate understanding and observation of the present can a clear idea of the past be devised by observing human nature in society. Understanding the past by thinking of present human society as a microcosm for historical civilisations can enable the historian to grasp – to a point – how the past happened. The rise and fall of states, revolutions and uprisings, the various activities and occupations of men, and the transformation societies and states go through are all useful to observe. Ibn Khaldun also warned that all historical records are liable to error because of the way the human mind receives and reflects on this record: 'Thought takes place by means of a power residing in the middle of his brain

---

108. Khaldūn and Issawi 1992, 26–28

which allows him to grasp the images of sensible objects and to turn them over in his mind, abstracting further images from them. Reflection consists of the manipulation of these images (behind sensation) by the mind, which breaks them up or recomposes them [to form other images] . . .'[109]

Between the classical period and the European Enlightenment, Arab scholars had a great curiosity about ancient Egypt. It is a common misconception that all Muslims considered cultures pre-dating Islam as *Jahiliya* ('ignorance') and hence altogether cancelled them from their knowledge. Western museum institutions echo this modern idea of radical Islam so as to validate keeping objects in their universalist collections.[110] Arabic medieval scholars and travellers wrote hundreds of manuscripts about ancient Egypt: several of these were documented in Okasha el-Daly's ground-breaking book, *Egyptology: The Missing Millennium* (2005), which for the first time brought to light more than a thousand 'missing' years of writing about ancient Egypt. El-Daly revealed that the first explorer to find gold treasure belonging to ancient Egypt was Ibn

109. Khaldûn et al. 2020, 364
110. Hanna 2022

Touloun in the ninth century CE. He used it to build his magnificent mosque in Sayyida Zainab in Cairo, along with other architectural projects. Realising the value of such hidden treasures, he banned individual excavations and insisted that participants in official excavations had to have official permission under the supervision of the state.[111] Treasure hunting manuscripts have been used since then to describe how to find tombs; many of them described how reaching archaeological sites entailed finding broken pottery, dog bones (possibly dog burials in the cult of Osiris, such as the site of Abu Sir el-Malek in Beni Suef) and other archaeological features.[112] However, treasure hunting was not the main focus of archaeological investigation, and it was frowned upon by many other Arab medieval scholars. Instead, Al-Mas'udi, Al-Suyuti, Al-Maqrizi and Dhu-al-Nun followed Islamic teachings, endeavouring to seek knowledge in all paths and understand ancient Egyptian language, culture, religion and science. Their rich accounts show their zeal for understanding the Great Pyramids, the Sphinx, the various temples, the language of the ancient Egyptians and

---

111. El-Daly 2005, 32
112. El-Daly 2005, 47

most importantly, the alchemical sciences. Al-Baghadady, who lived between the eleventh and twelfth century CE, wrote in his book *al-Ifada* about how he documented the information he could find about ancient Egypt through ethno-historical sources. He went to a number of different villages to ask the contemporary inhabitants about their inherited traditions, festivals and beliefs, then traced these to ancient Egyptian practices.[113] Another methodology that medieval Arab scholars used was trying to understand history by assimilating the oral history stories propagated into Arabic and North African epics. An example of such assimilation is the story of the conquests of Alexander the Great, which was called *Dhu al-Qarnin* (possibly after his iconographic association with the god Amun) in the Arabic oral tradition.[114] Medieval Arab scholars also believed that magic strongly connected the past and the present and sought to understand magical spells in Coptic in order to gather an idea of the practice in ancient Egypt. Postmodern archaeologists often use the social sciences to understand the past; Ibn Khaldun employed this thinking hundreds of years ago.

---

113. El-Daly 2005, 47
114. El-Daly 2005, 124–126

The French School of Egyptology v. the French School of Philosophy

Medieval Arab scholars saw ancient Egypt as a point on a timeline that continued to their own day, where the present interacted with the past. In contrast, French Egyptology progressed by presenting ancient Egypt as an entirely different entity from its modern-day counterpart. Despite French philosophy in the Age of Enlightenment and the nineteenth and twentieth centuries, French Egyptology has yet to incorporate these schools of thought into its theoretical or practical study of the discipline. French Egyptology was primarily built on the French school of Egyptology founded after Champollion deciphered the Rosetta Stone, but it did not find a shape until 1860 as a reaction to the firm establishment of the Berlin school. The French school focuses on objects and their interpretation, particularly at the Louvre and other French museums. The IFAO (Institut Français d'Archéologie Orientale) works mainly on consolidating the different concessions following the nineteenth- and early twentieth-century French monopoly of the Antiquities Service. Their monumental work, the *Cahier de Karnak*, has been beneficial for understanding the temple in documenting the descriptive work of the excavations carried out there over the years. Yet it has primarily been available only in French, inaccessible to the millions of Egyptians interested in understanding their past.

Unlike the restricted and conservative French Egyptology school, the French philosophical school has pioneered approaches incorporating social science and humanities. Juan Carlos Moreno García, in his article 'The Cursed Discipline',[115] describes the publication of Vercoutter's *L'Egypte et la vallée du Nil: De la fin de l'Ancien Empire à la fin du Nouvel Empire*[116] as embodying everything that is wrong with French Egyptology and Egyptology in general. Notwithstanding French claims to be the 'pioneers' of Egyptology – and their insistence that without their imperial efforts, the world would not have known ancient Egypt – French Egyptology today is stuck in pre-post-modernist thought.

Despite how mummified French Egyptology has become, French philosophers continue to inspire the discipline elsewhere. In *The Second Sex*, Simone de Beauvoir famously declared, 'One is not born, but rather becomes, a woman'[117] – illustrating the social construction of gender. She was also the first to

115. García 2014
116. Vercoutter and Vandersleyen 1992
117. De Beauvoir, Borde, and Malovany-Chevallier 2012

explain the concept of 'otherness' from a gender perspective and how many authors throughout history identified as 'anonymous' could have been women. She explored ideas of alienation and loss of agency in her writing, and her work was vital to evolving our understanding of gender roles in ancient societies.

A colleague of de Beauvoir, Maurice Merleau-Ponty (1908–61), is best known for his work on embodiment and phenomenology,[118] explaining in his books that humans experience the world not simply from a detached position, but rather through their bodies. His philosophical work has opened the door to many archaeological studies and changed perspectives on how ancient societies interacted with materials, environmental landscapes and social spaces.[119] His work on materiality looked at the role of objects and spaces in societies and how such interpretation intertwined with their craft and functionality, giving archaeologists new structures of thinking for interpreting those societies' material culture and landscape.[120] Ponty's work on the relation between temporality and history tries to explain that time is not a linear progression of disconnected

118. Merleau-Ponty 1962, 303–304
119. Shanks and Tilley 1996, 95
120. Tilley 2020

moments, but rather a unified whole, where the past is not entirely gone, and the future is not entirely separate, but both are intertwined with the present.[121]

Jean Baudrillard (1929–2007) created several theories that *should* have enabled Egyptology to evolve. Indeed, many of his works have influenced the study of archaeology and architecture, forming part of mainstream scholarship. In his first theory on simulacra and simulation, he explained that reality is dominated by signs, symbols and images that may entirely differ from the original. Archaeologists later employed this theory to analyse how ancient societies constructed and represented their realities.[122] They looked at how these constructions evolved, how these different systems working together were reinterpreted over time, and how archaeological practice is a simulacrum of the past in the present. Another of Baudrillard's theories that could be related to archaeological practice is that of 'hyper-reality', referring to a situation where the distinction between the real and the simulation does not exist. This work relates in particular to the massive French reconstruction projects in Saqqara and Karnak. In

121. Mazis 1992
122. Shanks and Tilley 1996, 105

Saqqara, Jean Philippe Lauer (1902–2001) spent his entire life at the cemetery, reconstructing the Djoser complex and presenting it as an absolute reality. His views on how to present archaeological sites are perhaps understandable – he belonged to a different generation, after all – yet his contemporary disciples, who continued the project in Saqqara, Karnak, Deir el-Medina and Tanis, have never looked back, continuing the same work with the same methodologies.

Jacques Derrida (1930–2004) argued that meaning is not innate to objects and texts but is produced through *différence* and *deferral*.[123] *Différence* is explained as the inherent difference that no two concepts, words or experiences are identical, while *deferral* is explained as meaning that the past is never fully understood, like a horizon that can never be truly reached. Archaeologists have adopted such ideas to provide multiple explanations as to how the interpretation of material culture is contingent upon the different historical contexts in which these objects were found. A second theory of Derrida's is *deconstruction*, a method using which he tried to expose contradictions and instabilities within texts and to challenge the assumptions and hierarchies

123. Derrida and Spivak 2013

on which they are based. This has been used widely by archaeologists to acknowledge the inherent incompleteness and fragmentation of the archaeological record, and how the past is always present through traces, echoes and assimilation.[124] Derrida also worked on the ethics of interpretation and the responsibility of the archaeologist, or philologist, to engage in reading and interpreting texts in ways that acknowledge the limitations of their understanding. Such ideas echo Ibn Khaldun's reflexive methods of our role in shaping the understanding of the past and the ethical implications of such responsibility.

The work of Michel Foucault (1926–84) focused on power discourse and the construction of knowledge. Foucault's main argument was that knowledge cannot be objective or neutral but is continuously produced within social and historical contexts through narrative. His ideas have been applied in archaeology to understand how the production of archaeological knowledge is shaped by contemporary social and political ideologies. Foucault's monumental book *L'Archaeologie De Savoir* (1969) argues for a method of analysing the pretexts and conditions through which historical narrative

---

124. Tilley 2014, 16–42

can be created.[125] The method has been used in archaeology to identify underlying power relations and to challenge the assumptions and biases that modern society has created with respect to the past.[126] Foucault emphasised that the relationship between power and knowledge is propagated through narrative rather than by individuals and institutions. Archaeologists have used this dynamic to legitimise power structures that control discipline and suppress alternative narratives of the past. From this idea, Foucault created the notion of *heterotopia*, commonly replicated in museums of objects representing the 'Other'.[127] In explaining *heterotopia*, Foucault describes how museums bring together objects from different historical periods, cultures and geographical locations, mixing different times with different spaces that do not exist in reality, thus creating a mirror unreal reflection of the past and perhaps the present by mixing the real with the imaginary. His work has profoundly influenced the humanities and social sciences and was the foundation for the post-modern thought that further shaped post-processual archaeological theories.

125. Foucault and Sheridan 1972
126. Foucault 1982
127. Foucault and Miskowiec 1986

French philosophy helped disciplines such as history to become, through the employment of social theory, a comprehensive social science, unlike Egyptology.[128]

The Berlin School v. the Frankfurt School

The Berlin school of Egyptology was viewed with jealousy by the French. Although it was developed relatively late, it was built on solid foundations through philanthropy and support from Alexander von Humboldt (1769–1859). Humboldt's aim was to unify the sciences, and he found that ancient Egypt provided an excellent opportunity to realise his ideas. He recognised the abilities of Karl Richard Lepsius, funding his early Egyptological training, and supported the promising research of Heinrich Brugsch.[129] Egyptology in Germany was characterised by continuous solid support from the Prussian government, especially after objects were brought back by Johan Heinrich von Minutoli (1772–1846). Minutoli excavated in Hermopolis-Al-Ashmounin in Minya and in Saqqara, where he discovered the entrance to the step pyramid. Yet according to the National Archive of Egypt, the only permit he

---

128. Iggers, Wang, and Mukherjee 2013, 257
129. Reid 2003, 41–42

acquired from Mehmet Ali dates to November 1820, putting all the objects he acquired for Germany and Switzerland (such as the mummy of Schepen Isis in St Gallen) in a contested position.[130] By 1870, Germany was taking the lead in Egyptology, not in the field like the French, but through the continuous concentration of German museums on texts and philology, resulting in the publishing of *Koptische Grammatik* in 1880.[131] Adolf Erman (1854–1937) can be seen as the true founder of the Berlin school, having fully recognised the direct relationship between the Ancient Egyptian language and other Afro-Asiatic languages. Unfortunately for Erman, he had Jewish ancestry despite being a Protestant. Under Nazi rule, he was stripped of his academic positions and honours.[132] Many Jewish Egyptologists found themselves in similar life-threatening situations, and fled Germany to the United States or Switzerland. Others committed suicide.

The Deutsches Archäologische Institut (DAI; German Archaeological Institute) was founded in 1907 by Ludwig Borchardt, who in 1905 had become

---

130. DWQ (Dār al-Wathāʾiq al-Qawmiyya The Sublime Porte, al-Māʾiyya al-Sāniya)
131. Jason Thompson 2015a, 152-154
132. Jason Thompson 2018, 200

a member of the Egyptology committee headed by Gaston Maspero.[133] Borchardt later became an agent for James Simon, a Jewish-German cotton trader who founded the Deutsche Orient-Gesellschaft (German Oriental Society) and was granted permission to excavate in Abusir and Amarna. On 6 December 1912, Borchardt discovered the famous bust of Nefertiti, bringing it to Germany with the aid of his benefactor, Simon, contrary to his concession contract and the *De Jure* law, which he was supposed to uphold as a member of the Egyptology committee.[134] He even hosted several private audiences at his house with the newly discovered bust. Still, by the end of World War I, he decided to donate the entire Amarna collection to the Berlin Museum on one condition – that if Egypt asked for the bust's return, it would be immediately repatriated.[135]

After the 1922 discovery of the tomb of Tutankhamun, Germany, out of imperial jealousy, decided to put the bust on display in the Berlin Museum. This alerted the Antiquities Service in Egypt and led to the immediate halting of all activities and

133. DWQ Dār al-Wathāʾiq al-Qawmiyya Majlis al-Wzraʾ w al-Nwẓar (The Ministers' Committee)

134. Hanna 2023, 1–5

135. Iskin 2022, 65–78

permissions, as well as the cancellation of concessions in Egypt held by the German Archaeological Institute. Negotiations started between Heinrich Schafer and Pierre Lacau under the supervision of the Royal Egyptian Legation in Berlin under the auspices of Hassan Nashaat Pasha and with support from Morcos Hanna Pasha, who had succeeded in assisting Saad Zaghloul in keeping the whole Tutankhamun collection in Egypt.

Negotiations in 1929 between the 'Scientific Institutions' resumed via diplomatic means in 1931, leading to the agreement of the Prussian government that there was an error in the division of files and that the Nefertiti bust should be repatriated. However, the Third Reich's government, led by Adolf Hitler, vetoed the Prussian government's decision, citing Hitler's admiration of the bust and proposing an Aryan ancestry for Nefertiti.[136] During the Nazi period, both Borchardt and Simon fled Germany in fear for their lives. After World War II, Egypt resumed the German Archaeological Institute's activities under Junker's direction. Nevertheless, German Egyptologists only returned to work in Egypt after 1952 when President Gamal Abdel Nasser wished to strengthen political

136. Barrowclough 2017

ties with Germany due to the Arab–Israeli conflict. Relations were later strained again during the 1967 war, leading to the closure of the DAI, which was put under the directorship of the Italian government – only to be reopened under Sadat.

The Frankfurt School of philosophy, founded on a Marxist critique of capitalism and alienation, can be divided into three phases: early, middle and late. It analysed how capitalism affects culture consciousness and subjectivity. Marx's class analysis was employed in historical and cultural studies, as were as his dialectical thinking and theory of alienation. Marxist archaeology was employed to emphasise how social relations and material capacities have shaped human society and history.[137] Such principles as materialism, social conflict and development shaped this study of archaeology. The Frankfurt School aimed to critique modern society and its dominant ideologies. One of its first-generation philosophers was Max Horkheimer, who co-authored a book with Theodor Adorno on the dialectic of enlightenment, critiquing the rise of mass culture in parallel to authoritarianism. Horkheimer and Adorno argued that our historical,

137. Spriggs 1984

social and personal context possibly shapes our understanding of the past. This resonates with the self-reflexive methodology of archaeology: how our personal biases, coupled with power dynamics, are directly embedded in our research. Horkheimer also critiqued the culture industry and its monopoly over the production of knowledge, stating that writing about the past selects particular interpretations and silences others. Horkheimer's work also encouraged interdisciplinarity in the humanities and social sciences between anthropology, sociology and history. Horkheimer and Adorno encouraged ethics and agency in terms of how social justice and human agency can interact with understanding the past.

Jürgen Habermas (1929–) built on his predecessors' work in discussing ideas concerning the public sphere and rational consensus. He emphasised the importance of a solid public sphere where diverse voices can engage in rational debate, inspiring multiple narratives about the past. He also advocated making knowledge accessible to wider audiences and promoting open and critical discussions about the ethical implications of archaeological practices and their impact on local communities. His work on universal pragmatics and intersubjectivity encourages understanding the intentions and communicative acts behind the creation and use of material culture to understand the researchers' positionality and biases when interpreting archaeological data, striving for intersubjectivity to understand multiple narratives about the past. The interpretation of the material culture says as much about the researcher as about the past. This was evident before Feminist archae-ology, where most material culture usually said to have been made by man and for man. For example, many of the early discoveries of birthing chairs in Deir el-Medina, the village of the workmen and their families who built the famous Valley of the Kings were first interpreted by men as a living room with chairs. The Frankfurt School inspired significant philosophical shifts within the humanities and social sciences, and it directly affected the evolution of history in Germany. The post-World War II break with traditional German narratives of the past trans-formed *historismus* into a meaningful social science. The influence of the Frankfurt School also reached the United States through Horkheimer and Adorno, who were forced to migrate before World War II.

By the mid-1970s, the critical school of study-ing the past launched a journal called *Geschichte und Gesellschaft* to incorporate such philosophical progressions.[138] Egyptology confined its progression to a closer focus on language through the production of Coptic and Egyptian dictionaries, and only in the last twenty years have German Egyptologists started publishing their research in languages other than German, causing their research to be more accessible to people who do not speak the language. However, in a recent publication, a book about ancient Nubia edited by the DAI's current director, all the chapters were written by Germans and a few other international scholars; none by a Nubian, either Egyptian or from Sudan. The book's subtitle states that it discusses Nubia right up until the twentieth century, yet Nubian voices remain silenced. On the other hand, Lara Weiss recently published a book exploring agency and ethics in her study of social relations in the history of Saqqara.[139] In a recent book by Allison Mickel analysing the anthropology of archaeological missions, she widely used Marx's theory of alienation and deemed the theory relevant[140] to everyday lives of workmen on Egyptian archaeological sites. Further work by Cornelia Kleinitz and Claudia Näser has also attempted to look at

138. Iggers, Wang, and Mukherjee 2013, 263–265
139. Weiss 2022, 19-25
140. Mickel 2021, 25-37

sociological aspects of modern societies between
Egypt and Sudan and their relations with the past.[141]

The British School v. British Theorists

Although there was no official British school or
institute of Egyptology, most British intervention
in Egypt came through direct colonial influence.
The British Museum's Department of Oriental
Antiquities was the only institution in Britain concerned with Egyptology in the nineteenth century. It
was built upon the spoils of war taken by Nelson's
army from the French. Sir E. A. Wallis Budge worked
in Egypt in the nineteenth century and was described
by the American Egyptologist James Henry Breasted
as 'Perhaps the most outstanding example of
incompetence in the whole range of British official
scholarship'.[142] What also made Budge the villain of
British archaeology was his illegal participation in
the antiquities trade, through which he succeeded
in selling items to the British Museum thanks to
shady connections with its trustees.

In 1893, the Victorian benefactor Amelia Edwards
established a professorship at the University College

---

141. Kleinitz and Näser 2011, 2012, 2013
142. Jason Thompson 2015a, 168

of London. Despite his poor teaching abilities, Sir
William Matthew Flinders Petrie took the professorship, and is now considered the father of scientific
archaeology in Egypt. He was also the first sponsor
of fieldwork through the Egypt Exploration Fund
(EEF) – a relic of Victorian society, primarily created
with the aim of furthering the agenda of biblical
archaeology. Petrie founded a niche for British
Egyptology to focus on material culture, supple-
menting German Egyptologists' work on language
and French Egyptologists' focus on art and religion.
However, bad faith between the British Museum, the
EEF and the University College of London caused
British Egyptology to stagnate.[143] This changed
when Francis Griffith, a self-educated Egyptologist
who worked at the British Museum, was granted a
readership in Egyptology at the University of Oxford
in 1901. Unlike Petrie, whose written word was
poor, Griffith was an excellent linguist, praised by
Egyptologists for his work on demotic and hieratic.
In addition, Margaret Murray (1863–1963), an
important figure in British archaeology, began
teaching Egyptology at the University College of
London. Many of her male colleagues said she won

143. Reid 2003, 179

the position through witchcraft, which she publicly confessed to practising, eventually publishing a book about it. She also published works on Egyptian and Coptic grammar and was interested in the anatomy of mummies. Later, she became one of the founding practitioners of Egyptology at the University of Manchester.

Petrie worked extensively in Egypt at Abydos, Amarna, Coptos, Dahshur, Fayum, Hierakonpolis, Naqada, Giza and El Qaw Al Kabir, and later in Palestine after he could no longer work in Egypt. He was accredited with the establishment of seriation theory, which provided relative dating for archaeological stratigraphy. (The theory proposed that material culture found deeper in the ground would be older than that found on the surface.) He used pottery dug from various trenches to create a historical timeline. He was also the first Egyptologist to use changes in style as a means of dating pottery and laid out a methodology for the drawing of pottery. However, Petrie also had racist ideas about non-European populations,[144] feeding the Coptic communities his theories by telling them they were the purest descendants of the ancient Egyptians

---

144. Challis 2013

and, indeed, that they were almost European. He wrote: 'A Coptic village is clean and well swept, the women sitting at work in the doorways and chatting across the street. It is on the level of a civilised Mediterranean land, and not like the filthy confusion of a Mohammedan village. . . Egypt will never be a civilised land till it is ruled by the Copts – if ever'.[145]

Processual archaeology, sometimes referred to as new archaeology or scientific archaeology, first gained traction in the 1960s and 1970s. It was primarily concerned with scientific methodologies: processual archaeologists sought to apply statistics and data analysis to the examination of ancient cultures. To study how earlier societies operated and adapted to their surroundings, it also strongly emphasised the understanding of cultural systems. Areas of interest included social organisation, trade, subsistence techniques, and how civilisations adapt to their cultural surroundings. Processual archaeology examines changes in climate and resource availability in order to comprehend the evolution of societies over time. Its leading pioneers were Sir Colin Renfrew and David Clarke. Processual archaeology emphasises scientific rigour

---

145. Petrie 2013, 223–224

and objectivity and attempts to explain past human development through environmental and social processes. This was a real challenge to the previous descriptive methodologies of cultural history and introduced systematic thinking to the field of archaeological inquiry.[146]

In the 1980s, as a response to the processual school, Ian Hodder and Christopher Tilley developed a theory of post-processual archaeology. It advocated a more subjective and interpretive approach, against the strong objectivism of the processual school. Their work has emphasised the role of meaning-making, social agency and the inclusion of multiple narratives in understanding the past.[147] The result from the late twentieth century was the evolution of landscape archaeology by Timothy Taylor and Tilley, who explored the relationship between ecosystems and human societies through phenomenological approaches to the understanding of landscape meanings and interactions via the new technological advances of Geographical Informational Systems (GIS) and Spatial Analysis. Following post-processualism,

---

146. Renfrew and Bahn 2020
147. Ian Hodder 2012a, 2012b; I. Hodder 1992; Ian Hodder 1995, 2006, 2016; Ian Hodder and Hutson 2003; Tilley 1997, 1990, 2014, 2020

critical archaeology schools of thought came to light in the late twentieth century.

Building on post-processualism, British archaeologists like Christopher, Chippendale and Rodney Harrison engaged in understanding the power dynamics of colonialism, critically assessing the role of archaeology in understanding contemporary historical narratives and the evolution of critical heritage studies through discussion of ethics, representation and social justice in archaeological practice.[148] This led to the evolution of public and community archaeology in the United Kingdom under the aegis of Stephanie Moser and Yannis Hamilakis.[149] These advances in archaeology trickled down to Egyptology. For example, in David Wengrow's recent publication *Rethinking Civilizations*,[150] he challenges the traditional Eurocentric narrative arising from urbanism and social hierarchy. He brings archaeological evidence from a range of societies worldwide, and fluidly connects them to show the presence of complex social and political structures in non-urban settings.

148. Harrison 2013
149. Moser et al. 2002; Hamilakis 2005, 2012, 2016b, 2011; Hamilakis 2014; Hamilakis 2016a, 2018; Hamilakis and Duke 2016; Hamilakis, Pluciennik, and Tarlow 2012; Hamilakis and Theou 2013; Hamilakis and Yalouri 1996
150. Graeber and Wengrow 2021

He argues between simplistic descriptive interpretations of material culture and advocates studying the
past through social practices, meanings and power
relations. This approach shows the agency people
can have in shaping their societies and environments,
a key idea for Egyptologists today. Wengrow draws
upon the philosophies of Thomas Hobbes, Jean-
Jacques Rousseau, Adam Smith, Ibn Khaldun and
Sigmund Freud. Such engagement with social theory
made his publication cutting-edge in archaeology.
Other British Egyptologists who have tried to bring in
similar narratives are Richard Parkinson[151], Stephan
Quirke[152] and Penelope Wilson.[153]

The Italian School v. Italian Theorists

Besides its celebrated Italian adventurer, the 'Great'
Belzoni, Italy had dedicated scholars such as Ippolito
Rosellini, who helped with the initial decipherment
of the Ancient Egyptian language through his
work on demotic and served as a link between
Champollion and Lepsius. In the nineteenth century,
Grand Duke Leopold II was the Tuscan sponsor of
the French–Tuscan Expedition to Egypt. Egyptology

---

151. R. B. Parkinson 2009
152. Quirke 2013
153. Pennington et al. 2020

in Italy was focused on collecting objects mainly for the Florence and Turin museums, alongside smaller provincial institutions and private collectors who saw the ownership of Egyptian objects as a status symbol.[154] Italian Egyptological praxis in Egypt at the beginning of the twentieth century focused largely on Greco-Roman archaeology. In 1892, Italians finally took over the direction of the Greco-Roman Museum in Alexandria. Giuseppe Botti and Evaristo Breccia excavated in Greater Alexandria, aiming to explore Greco-Roman layers of history. Egyptologist Ernesto Schiaparelli (1856–1928) shifted the focus towards Egyptian excavations, digging throughout the country between 1903 and 1920. His most famous finding was the tomb of Nefertari in the Valley of the Queens in Luxor. He also directed the Egyptian section of the museums in Florence and later Turin.

The figures who established Italian Egyptology were Sergio Donadoni in Rome and Michela Schiff Giorgini in Pisa, who worked on salvaging the temple of Soleb in Nubia. The Italian School has since continued to focus largely on the interpretation of Egypt's Greco-Roman archaeology, with a particular emphasis on in Fayyum,

154. Piacentini 2021, 372

where the late Edda Bresciani (1930–2020) transferred interdisciplinary work in Italy of heritage site management to the Egyptological works in Fayyum. Since its privatisation, attempts have been made to paint the Turin Museum in a more progressive light by allowing visitors of Egyptian and Arab descent to visit for free. However, the museum has yet to face the legacy of the thousands of unprovenanced, looted objects that are still displayed in their collection.

In his letters from prison, Antonio Gramsci (1891–1937) discusses his central concept and framework, that of hegemony. He analyses how dominant groups keep their power by employing cultural and ideological methods such as monuments, symbols, and publications reflected in material culture. Gramsci also coined the term 'subaltern', whereby historians could explore the voices and experiences of marginalised communities often absent from the official archaeological narrative. His ideas inspired archaeologists to consider the agency and resistance of such communities and how they are expressed in material traces. His concept of historical materialism examined the relationship between social formations and material conditions and how changes in production, class, relations and power dynamics can be extrapolated from archaeological evidence.

Gramsci's concepts were applied to a critique of traditional descriptive archaeological practices and interpretations to highlight their biases and imbalances. His work inspired archaeologists to produce multi-vocal interpretations of the past by embracing diverse perspectives on material remains, acknowledging the role of agency and subjectivity in the archaeological records. His work also inspired ethno-archaeological research, combining anthropology and archaeology to examine how living communities and their material practices can give us insights into past societies and how meaning can be encoded in material culture. Others used his work to examine the space between elite and everyday settlements in an effort to understand power dynamics. People also worked with his concepts to deconstruct colonial practices in archaeology relating to indigenous cultures and material landscapes.[155]

The work of Umberto Eco (1932–2016) provides valuable insights into archaeological investigations. His work *Semiotics and the Philosophy of Language* entails a detailed analysis of the complexities of interpretation, the power of signs and symbols and the role of the observer in constructing meaning. His work on science systems and material culture

---

155. Kelley 1992

analysed archaeological objects, monuments and landscape systems to provide an interpretive methodology for objects, buildings and landscapes and how they communicate messages about identity, power and belief systems. And his essays in *Travels in Hyperreality* provide ideas for interpreting material culture beyond the practical: by understanding the symbolic dimensions embedded in forms, materials and decoration. He also stresses the fictional nature of any archaeological reconstruction, and the fallibility of historical records – and how this can inform archaeologists' critical reflection on how they construct the past.

The American School and the Birth of Gender and Post-colonial Theories

American Egyptology was initially based on attempts to confirm biblical truths and to justify slavery and belief in the inferiority of the Black race.[156] Greek and Roman civilisation were usually employed in the justification of slavery – all great civilisations had had slaves. Evidence from the material culture and from a few books written in the nineteenth century showed ancient Egyptians too were highly sophisticated and

---

156. Thompson Vol 2, Chapter 10 Footnote 23

civilised. This presented a complex ethical problem to most Americans as to how Egypt, located as it was in Africa, created such a remarkable civilisation. George Glidden was the first Egyptologist who tried to answer such a tricky question. His first publication, *Ancient Egypt,* in 1843, was designed to prove that Egyptians were a branch of the Caucasian race, putting the Americans at peace with how they dealt with the slavery problem.[157] The Exodus accounts of the flight from Egypt also provided necessary support for the American Christian Zionist movement, and America took part in the Egypt Exploration Society alongside Britain to produce knowledge about Egypt, until fights between the sponsors led to the disbandment of the society.

Through the University of Chicago, James Henry Breasted (1865–1935) was a member of the Berlin school of Egyptology, until his eventual return to the United States as a full-time professor at the University of Chicago. Breasted translated ancient records, usually citing himself as he claimed he could not trust other translations, leading other Egyptologists in turn to doubt these Breasted's work. Later in his career, he obtained the necessary funds

---

157. 204–205

from the University of Chicago to continue working in Egypt. One of his followers, George A. Reisner (1867–1942), also completed his studies in Germany. Combining Petrie's methodology with some German methods and his own American practicality, he developed good practice in his work in Giza and Nubia. He eventually became a full-time professor at Harvard University.

Both Breasted and Reisner established the oldest institutions working on Egyptology in America. In 1948, the American Research Center of Egypt (ARCE) was established in Boston, and an Egyptian branch founded in 1951. It was designed to help North American scholars in Egypt and later extended its work to the country's various historical periods, its Coptic, Islamic and contemporary heritage. ARCE was not just concerned with study; it also facilitated study tours for Americans wanting to learn more about ancient Egypt from the experts. Despite America's lack of colonial heritage in Egypt, Americans have exercised cultural imperialism over Egypt's past. American Egyptology was part of a liberal arts movement in education within the United States. It helped its evolution and enabled it to catch up with related disciplines such as anthropology, history and social sciences. But while it employed theories and methods from such disciplines to a certain extent, it did not fully embrace them until recently.

Edward Said was a Palestinian American, a friend of Michel Foucault, who in his monumental philosophical work *Orientalism* deconstructed the Western narrative about the East in a post-structuralist, post-modernist school of thought. Said attributes the origin of Orientalism to Napoleon's French campaign in Egypt.[158] He deconstructs the imperial powers fighting over the East and attributes the Arab-Israeli conflict to colonialism in America, and warns against using binary opposition, where archaeological narratives usually set the rational West against the irrational East. He critically examines such a binary overview of the world in the anthropological identification of the 'Other'. Said is credited with originating the first post-colonial theories on the power dynamics and production of knowledge through the unmasking of colonial agendas that legitimise Western dominance and control. Said's work also critiqued Western-centric frameworks on how archaeological methods and interpretations affected Western biases and epistemology. His invitation to the humanities and social sciences was to move

---

158. E. Said 1995

beyond the exoticism of Eastern cultures that often sensationalised and 'othered' them. Said strove for respectful, nuanced representations that avoid perpetuating stereotypes and misinterpretations, aiming to create a meaningful understanding between the East and the West.

Noam Chomsky, an ardent critic of post-modernism, put forward the idea of *universal grammar* (UG): the theory that all human languages contain innate cognitive structures which shape how people communicate. Chomsky, an American Jew, agreed with Said on some aspects of Orientalism, and his work always advocated reflexivity and critique.[159] Said and Chomsky were also the first scholars to portray an image of a college professor who could engage with questions and conversations from everyday life.

Judith Butler has revolutionised our view of how gender was read in the past by deconstructing gender binaries and identities. Her work challenges the traditional interpretations of gender roles in past societies;[160] through it, archaeologists are reconsidering burial practices, settlement patterns and material culture to uncover the diversity of gender expressions

---

159. E. W. Said 1975
160. Butler 2004

in ancient societies that move beyond biological determinism. She emphasises how gender performance can be a way for archaeologists to understand how gender was constructed and enacted through social practices, rituals and material culture. Her work is also coupled with earlier phenomenological ideas of embodiment through analysing material expressions of gender, such as how bodies were adorned, modified and presented. The products of material cultures, such as clothing, jewellery and other objects, can help archaeologists understand how past societies constructed and performed gender. Her work has also focused on encouraging archaeologists to investigate how spaces were designed to reinforce or subvert gender norms.[161] This can be read by analysing the organisation of particular settlements, burial sites, ritual spaces and gendered artefacts. Butler's work has also helped examine power dynamics in gender relations and how inequalities and hierarchies were maintained in past societies. Besides understanding social division, class and power, archaeologists look through Butler's lens to explore how gender intersected with all these fields.[162]

---

161. Butler 2014
162. Meskell 1991; Joyce 2004; Hanna 2021; Cooney 2018; Ayad 2009; Matić 2012, 2016

The Road Not Taken

The school of Egyptian Egyptology lagged due to the reasons mentioned in Part 1, where the only Egyptologists' positions given to Egyptians were menial: they were often asked to discipline the locals, rather than produce Egyptology themselves. Indigenous Egyptology tried to follow the different schools, so Egyptians were sent to study at different universities abroad and returned with various methodologies. In 1952, when Egyptians took control of the Antiquities Service, the knowledge stayed in Western hands despite the attempts at a local production of knowledge. The Egyptian Archaeology Department was created at Cairo University, previously known as Fuad I University, in 1925 and became a college in 1970. Many foreign instructors taught at the department until it became entirely Egyptian after 1952. Yet the 1952 Egyptian government has never fully restored agency for Egyptian Egyptologists to write about their past. Post-colonial Egyptology continued to alienate Egyptians, with the governance of heritage spaces favouring foreign archaeological missions and tourists. Knowledge about ancient Egypt has continued to be produced in Western circles and in languages the general Egyptian public could not read. Despite the department producing many fine Egyptologists with world class scholarship, a clear identifiable school of Egyptology was never created. Most Egyptologists, myself included, have preferred to publish in English rather than Arabic in order to be accessible to the academic community. Selim Hassan and Ahmed Fakhry have tried to publish extensively in Arabic, but their publications are outdated today.

Egyptian Egyptology could not form a distinct school primarily due to a lack of state excavation funding; most funding for excavation, site management and conservation comes from foreign entities. The few Egyptian missions are either Egyptian in name only or have individual financial support, such as the work of Cairo University in Saqqara. This has crippled the evolution of indigenous Egyptology and kept it dependent on foreign funding.

Despite this, several Egyptian Egyptologists have made breakthroughs. They include Fayza Haikal, who founded a department of Egyptology at the American University in Cairo and advocated the road that Ahmed Kamal had begun: studying the ancient Egyptian languages through Egyptian Arabic, as well as looking for ancient Egypt through the anthropological lens of cultural continuity and assimilation.[163] The great work by Dr Mohamed Abdel Maqsoud in discovering Tharou in Eastern Qantara, as well as his excavations along the Ways of Horus, have provided Egyptology with some important puzzle pieces. Today, many Egyptian Egyptologists – such as the late Ramadan el-Badri Hussein in Saqqara – have succeeded in producing state-of-the-art scholarship. Yet on an institutional level in Egypt, there has been no proper sponsorship of an indigenous school of Egyptology.

Taha Hussein was the first to call for the decolonisation of Egyptology. He was a prominent critic of Western domination of culture and Eurocentric ideas about ancient Egypt. Through his book *The Future of Culture in Egypt*, he tried to bring to light the marginalised indigenous voices of Egypt.[164] Hussein believed that cultural exchange and dialogue would encourage Egyptologists to engage in diverse perspectives on Egyptology by acknowledging the limitations of Western knowledge frameworks.[165] He also advocated the philosophy of the non-linear past and called for a more nuanced understanding of ancient Egypt through its intertwinement with the

---

163. Haikal 2003; Yusuf and Haikal 2003
164. Ahmed 2021, 23
165. Ahmed 2021, 85

Coptic and Islamic periods. In his view, this was the road map for a holistic understanding of Egyptian culture and identity across space and time. During Hussein's tenure as dean at Fuad I University, he created the Institute of Egyptian and Islamic Archaeology during the 1930–31 academic year, and helped find funding for the department, allowing it to start independent excavations including those at the pyramid of Queen Khentkawes in Giza and the Greco-Roman site in Tuna el-Gebel.

Egyptology and the Social Sciences

At the Lady Wallis Budge Symposium which took place at the University of Cambridge on 25–26 July 2017, a meeting was held to analyse the intersection of Egyptology with other disciplines, particularly anthropology.[166] This was not the first such event: in 1979, Kent Weeks and Manfred Beitak edited a volume of five essays on Egyptology and the social sciences, which discussed how Egyptology could be transformed from an area of study to a fully-fledged discipline within the humanities and social sciences.[167] The essays were a good start despite some of them

---

166. Howley and Nyord 2018
167. Weeks and Bietak 1979

not discussing the exact purpose for which the book was made. In 2011, John Baines wrote 'Egyptology and the Social Sciences: Thirty Years On', in which he discussed how Egyptology has remained an area of study, as opposed to an established discipline. Baines compares the position of Egyptology to that of anthropology, particularly after the employment of the theories of Emile Durkheim.[168] In 2014, Juan Carlos Moreno García wrote a book chapter in which he called Egyptology 'the cursed discipline', lamenting the apathy of Egyptologists who are content with keeping their field as a distinct or peculiar discipline.[169] García deconstructed the contemporary Egyptological narrative of 'Eternal Egypt', and noted how, almost a century later, we are still beholden to Carter's 'wonderful things'.[170] This mummification of the discipline has restricted its study to topics relating to the 'official', 'elite', 'prestige' and 'religious', disregarding other matters that represented the wider Egyptian social spectrum.[171]

In 2022, Claus Jurman published an article on post-colonial Egyptology that started with this

---

168. Baines 2011, 579
169. García 2014, 51
170. García 2014, 52
171. García 2014, 54

overarching statement: 'While Egyptology is gradually trying to come to terms with its problematic
past, it is, in an almost reckless manner, turning a
blind eye to its problematic present, thereby risking
forfeiting its future'.[172] For the first time, real contemporary problems were raised, such as the use,
ignored by Egyptologists, of illegal child labour on
excavations, as well as how current geopolitics are
affecting Egyptology. In 2023, an article by Matić
and Langer attempted to deconstruct post-colonial
attempts in Egyptology.[173]

Return to Belzoni's Circus

'Popular culture and the media consider Egyptology
as a provider of entertainment and illusion for
our rather gloomy present'.[174] In the past twenty
years, Egyptology has been plagued by populist
showmanship mixed with science, sometimes with
pseudoscience, to attract Western tourism rather
than producing knowledge for the discipline's
development or for the benefit of local communities.
Such activities, displayed on the screen, have no
respect for the human body's dignity, and human

172. Jurman 2022
173. Langer and Matić 2023
174. García 2014, 54

remains are violated in a Victorian fashion ceremony of unwrapping mummies. Such 'spectacularisation' of Egyptology continues the heritage of the colonial past: wearers of Indiana Jones hats with neocolonialist agendas.[175] This tendency is encouraged by many Western archaeologists who indulge in cosplay and pose on archaeological sites with pith helmets and whips.[176] Their showmanship speaks of the gold, the kings and queens, the secrets and the recycled discoveries. Such activities do nothing but harm, for they fuel the antiquities market with uncontrolled waves of illicit excavations that use children's agile bodies to go into narrow shafts in search of objects, activities in the course of which some lose their lives for the sake of a few pounds.[177] This spectacularisation was not only practised by the previous director of the Supreme Council of Antiquities, Zahi Hawass, who faced corruption charges after the 2011 revolution.[178] The directorship of the Supreme Council under Mustafa Waziri has continued the same work under the pretext of marketing for tourism. The current excavations in Saqqara headed by Waziri use

---

175. Hanna 2019
176. Blouin, Hanna, and Bond 2020
177. Ikram and Hanna 2013; Hanna 2013, 2015; Jarus 2016
178. Marchant 2011

bulldozers to clear stratigraphic layers of history, bringing out objects to display without corresponding academic publication. Whole tombs have been cut and displaced from Sohag and Saqqara to be put in museums, disregarding the Venice Charter.[179] Medieval and modern historical layers have been wiped out to create an illusionary, imagined space for archaeology – the strongest example being the destruction of historical layers around the Avenue of Sphinxes in Luxor, under the pretext of creating an 'Open-air Museum'.[180] These practices destroy a site's archaeology and history, regressing the discipline to that of the nineteenth-century adventurers and antiquities traders, and severely curtailing the advances that Egyptian Egyptology has tried to make in recent times.

---

179. The Venice Charter was adopted internationally in 1964 to regulate conservation procedures for monuments, historical buildings and archaeological sites. Its goal is to preserve the cultural heritage for future generations through proper conservation and preservation procedures. The charter puts a monument's authenticity as its main conservation ethos, using original materials and original design while respecting the historical value of the monument. It focuses on minimal intervention where a clear distinction between original and newly added elements must be highlighted.
180. Kenawi 2024

Part III
The Future

In this concluding part, I reflect on my career as an Egyptologist through discussions with colleagues and peers. Perhaps through such discussions and reflections, we can try to envision the 'Future of Egyptology'.

As a student, I was taught nothing of the political context of archaeology in Egypt, the grossly unequal conditions in which excavations took place, or the racism that was inherent to Egyptology – a racism that was, in fact, its reason for existence. Little has changed today in school or university curricula, with some encouraging exceptions and initiatives. It is slow progress, often met with reactionary responses or, worse, silence. What Egyptians, of every social level and identity, have to say about their history remains marginalised, as are they. In Western European thought that emerged over the eighteenth century, the modern inhabitants of Egypt were deemed incapable of understanding its ancient past, much less appreciating and caring for it.[181]

A Phenomenology of Egyptology

The future of Egyptology is best understood by navigating the challenges faced by the various stakeholders in the discipline today. Colleagues I have spoken with have assessed the current state of research production, explored its representation in popular culture and envisioned hopes and expectations for its future. Through the voices of practitioners in the field, insights are gained into the multifaceted challenges that Egyptology grapples with, unravelling its cultural impact on society. Like any scientific discipline, Egyptology faces many challenges that shape its trajectory.

Ibrahim Saweros, associate professor of Coptic Studies at Sohag University, draws attention to the need for excavations, often influenced by ideological agendas and monopolised by a select few, to be given proper academic publication. This challenge

---

181. Riggs 2021, 67

not only hinders the dissemination of knowledge but also raises questions about the authenticity and inclusivity of archaeological narratives. Mahmoud Abdel Hafez, Professor of Inorganic Conservation at Cairo University, further underscores the financial constraints that impede Egyptological pursuits. The scarcity of resources for archaeological excavations, coupled with the predominant involvement of foreign missions, brings to light the broader issue of dependence on external support. While foreign expertise is undoubtedly valuable, the lack of substantial local investment raises questions about the ownership and benefit-sharing of Egypt's rich cultural heritage. Saleh Abdelrassoul, one of the grandchildren of the famous Abdelrassoul of Deir el-Bahari Cache and a student of Egyptian archaeology at the College of Archaeology and Cultural Heritage, delves into the post-colonial complex, shedding light on the disparity in the attention given to Egyptian Egyptologists compared to their foreign counterparts. This raises critical questions about equity, recognition, and the potential perpetuation of colonial dynamics within the field.

The theme of unequal recognition is echoed by Shahinaz Abdelrassoul, another of the grandchildren of Abdelrassoul and also a student of

Egyptian archaeology at the College of Archaeology and Cultural Heritage, who contends that foreign archaeologists often enjoy higher esteem than their Egyptian counterparts. The call to replace foreign missions with Egyptian ones underscores the demand for equitable representation and the need to empower local expertise. Ahmed Eissa, Professor Emeritus of Egyptian Archaeology at Cairo University, addresses a multifaceted challenge: financial constraints, archaeological awareness, and the entry of non-specialised individuals into the field. The struggle to balance economic considerations with the preservation of cultural heritage is evident, reflecting broader societal attitudes towards archaeology and antiquities.

The state of Egyptological research production further complicates the narrative. Saweros provides a global perspective, pointing out that Egyptian Egyptological production still falls below international standards. This global comparison raises questions about the factors that contribute to this disparity and the need for strategic interventions to bridge the gap. Hassan Abou el-Nasr, a teaching assistant in the Ancient Egyptian language, critiques the need for more innovative ideas and improved content in current archaeological research. His perspective draws attention to the qualitative aspect of research production, emphasising the importance of contributing original knowledge to the field rather than pursuing publication in order to gain academic credentials. In his assessment of current research, Eissa highlights the repetition of old information and laments the missed opportunities for utilising recent discoveries. This raises questions about the efficiency of knowledge transfer mechanisms within the field, urging a revaluation of how new findings are incorporated into the existing body of Egyptological knowledge.

Khaled Gharib, Professor of Greco-Roman Archaeology at Cairo University, succinctly characterises the state of current research as 'dreadful', encapsulating a sentiment shared by many within the field. The lack of content and ideas and the inferior quality of scientific material underscore the urgent need to reinvigorate research practices. The assessment of Ibrahim Badr, Associate Professor of Organic Conservation at Misr International University, aligns with the prevailing sentiment, emphasising Egypt's terrible state of archaeological research. His brief commentary encapsulates a collective frustration with the current trajectory of research production, prompting a critical reflection on the systemic issues contributing to this state of affairs.

Abdel Hafez provides a more nuanced perspective, acknowledging the efforts of some researchers amidst the challenges. The juxtaposition of weak scientific research with the need for easy access to archaeological objects underscores the interconnected nature of challenges within Egyptology. The call for more support, both financial and logistical, reflects a plea for systemic change to uplift the field.

Beyond the academic realm, the representation of Egyptology in popular culture becomes a lens through which the broader society engages with the discipline. Saweros notes the prevalence of 'magical exploration'[182] in popular culture, drawing attention to a legacy that often eschews serious study. This observation raises questions about the role of public perception in shaping the trajectory of Egyptology and the need for a more informed and nuanced understanding. Abou el-Nasr focuses on the potential embedded in customs and traditions derived from ancient Egypt. His call to study these echoes emphasises the untapped cultural wealth that Egyptology can

---

182. Since the medieval period, special magical practices have been widely used in Egyptian society to look for tombs and archaeological sites. For further readings, this article at *al-Ahram* newspaper provides some interesting thoughts: gate.ahram.org.eg/News/3635293.aspx

contribute to contemporary society. The challenge lies not only in preserving these customs but also in decoding and disseminating their significance. Eissa provides a sociocultural perspective, highlighting the deep-rooted influence of ancient Egypt on Egyptian behaviour, language and traditions. His insights shed light on the intangible cultural heritage to which Egyptology contributes, emphasising the need to recognise and appreciate these connections in the broader cultural consciousness.

Gharib's perspective on the vibrancy of Egyptian popular culture adds a positive dimension to the discourse. Recognising Egypt as a civilisation that has had no dark stage, he emphasises the role of art and literature as expressions invented by ancient Egyptian civilisation. This viewpoint challenges the prevailing narrative of decline and stagnation within the field, encouraging a more holistic understanding of Egyptology's cultural impact. Badr's acknowledgement of ancient Egyptian influences in popular culture, albeit without systematic study, hints at a missed opportunity. The lack of comprehensive research into the cultural permeation of ancient Egypt raises questions about the discipline's engagement with broader societal narratives and the potential for enriching public understanding.

The role of Egyptology in fostering cross-cultural understanding emerges as a recurring theme. Saweros notes its potential as a crucible where diverse cultures meet but points out the prevailing lack of equality in these encounters. This observation prompts a critical reflection on the dynamics of collaboration within the field and the need for a more inclusive and equitable approach. Gharib expands on this theme, emphasising Egyptology's role in bridging cultures, particularly between North and West Africa. The call for a common understanding of the customs and traditions of each society underscores the potential for Egyptology to serve as a mediator in cross-cultural dialogues. Abdel Hafez takes a historical perspective, highlighting Egyptology's role in cultural partnerships throughout Egyptian history. The call for museums to showcase common the material culture of civilisations – i.e. the objects of day-to-day life – further emphasises the potential for artefacts to provide shared cultural experiences. This perspective challenges an often-isolated approach to cultural heritage, encouraging a more interconnected understanding. Badr underscores Egyptology's unique position as an incubating environment for diverse sciences, fostering international cooperation. His emphasis on the interdisciplinary nature of

Egyptology as a catalyst for collaboration across various scientific disciplines highlights the potential for the field to contribute to historical understanding and contemporary scientific advancements.

Amidst the challenges and critiques, a collective hope for the future of Egyptology resonates among these voices. Saweros articulates the need for sufficient funding, equal opportunities for researchers, and legislation to govern foreign institutions working on archaeological and conservation projects. This multi-faceted approach recognises that sustainable progress in Egyptology requires a comprehensive revaluation of the systemic factors contributing to its challenges. Gharib envisions Egyptology as a practical science with implications for society, branching into various fields. His vision challenges the dichotomy between theoretical and applied sciences, emphasising the potential for Egyptology to contribute both to academic knowledge and societal advancement. Eissa's hope for improved financial support for Egyptian missions and enhanced scientific publishing after discoveries are made reflect a desire for a more robust and equitable distribution of resources. The acknowledgement of the competence of Egyptian archaeologists emphasises the need for recognition and support for local expertise. Abdel Hafez calls for international cooperation and financial support to complete archaeological discoveries and protect artefacts. His plea reflects an awareness of the global interconnectedness of Egyptology and the need for collaborative efforts to preserve and disseminate cultural heritage.

Abdel Hafez sheds light on the challenges inherent in accessing Egyptological knowledge, citing difficulties in the acquisition of scientific sources and publications on ancient Egyptian civilisation. This challenge is not only a reflection of limited access but also underscores the importance of democratising knowledge within the field. The barriers to entry for enthusiasts and scholars hinder the democratisation of Egyptological expertise and contribute to the perpetuation of exclusive narratives. His suggestions for improvement encompass a holistic approach to knowledge dissemination. Spreading the culture of reading among the public, distributing publications and other educational materials on public occasions, public transportation and within state agencies are proposed strategies to bridge the knowledge gap. This grassroots approach recognises the importance of public engagement and emphasises the role of Egyptology in fostering a sense of belonging to the broader cultural heritage. Creating visual and audio channels dedicated to Egyptology would be a pragmatic step towards making the discipline more accessible. Abdel Hafez's proposal aligns with contemporary trends in digital media consumption, recognising the potential for visual and audio content to engage a broader audience. The emphasis on integrating Egyptology into educational institutions in Egypt, including schools, colleges and public libraries, addresses the need.

As for the long-term future of Egyptology, divergent perspectives emerge, painting a complex picture of the discipline's trajectory. Saweros anticipates a potential decline in Egyptology's significance compared to emerging disciplines. This projection prompts questions about the adaptability of Egyptology in the face of evolving scientific paradigms and the need for strategic planning to ensure its continued relevance. Badr envisions technology as crucial in changing foundational concepts in Egyptian heritage. This foresight highlights the dynamic nature of scientific inquiry within Egyptology and the potential for technological advancements to reshape our understanding of ancient Egypt. Abdel Hafez, in his optimistic prediction, foresees Egyptology's growing importance, penetrating other sciences and creating modern industries. This visionary perspective challenges the notion of stagnation within the field, presenting

Egyptology as a dynamic and evolving discipline with the potential to influence contemporary scientific and industrial landscapes.

Towards a Critical Egyptology

The idea of 'decolonisation' has multiple connotations in the setting of museums, academic publications, archaeological sites, and even in the language of activists and politicians; there is no single definition for it, either conceptually or practically. Decolonisation has been used, paradoxically, both to fight the intrinsic Western bias of museum collections and Egyptological practice, and as a brand to re-establish institutions' legitimacy and relevance to audiences. Decolonisation has different meanings in different contexts and can mean enabling indigenous scholars, empowering local communities, or rewriting historical narratives or inclusive policies for heritage management. However, at the same time, post-colonial practices have sometimes been more alienating to the 'subaltern' (in a Gramscian sense) in how they continue not to be allowed to engage with their heritage, thus perpetuating an inherent legacy of colonialism. If ancient Egypt is to survive in the future, as many of us have experienced in the field, Egyptology must be thoroughly engaged with sustainable community development. Communities that are apathetic to the archaeological investigation will loot, seize land and neglect important sites. Losing the archaeological context of our past will lead to substantial cultural attrition.[183] Such attrition can only be stopped by shifting back archaeological investigation to the Nile Delta, as has been the case since 1952, through working with the Sustainable Development Goals (SDGs) of the 2030 UN agenda. Archaeological field investigation must be part of development plans forged with communities and based on their developmental needs. This can only be done by engaging Egyptology more with the social sciences, with international bodies and Egyptian policymakers, to change the nature of archaeological practice, both in Egypt and abroad, so that it becomes inclusive and sustainable. Indigenous communities need to benefit directly from archaeological practices; a sustainable cultural, intellectual and economic relationship must be the foundation for any site investigation.

Although the world's first museums were in Ur in Iraq and Alexandria in Egypt, modern museums are embedded in European modernity. Unlike those found in Ur and Alexandria, they express a perception of how the West sees 'the other', or

183. Hanna 2020

colonised populations. The 'other' for these museums represents a reference for identifying identity and difference to be subdued. By conquering other peoples and assimilating their cultural heritage, the West built its modern identity based on the hierarchisation of different forms of knowledge. Such museums and Egyptological organisations in the West (and mainly in Europe) were and still are funded and sponsored by national institutions. For a long time, museums and archaeological institutes competed politically over the ancient Egyptian past(s). The main axes of Egyptological inquiry were thus shaped by nation-states, uniquely positioned to determine which activities were to be funded and supported, regarded as culturally significant, or simply of imperialist or colonialist interest. Decolonising Western Egyptian collections is not only about repatriating cultural material artefacts, but also repairing past injustices, beginning with a focus on people rather than objects. This process requires communities' involvement in the museum practices that historically alienated them.

The ethical code of museums worldwide is changing, and galleries are looking closely at their collections, trying to wipe out the cultural and material violence that enabled such collections to be amassed. Decolonising the Western museum is not only about the restitution and repatriation of objects such as the Rosetta Stone, the Nefertiti Bust or the Dendera Zodiac, but is intended to restore agency to Egyptians, enabling them to produce knowledge about their past.

In Egyptology today, there is a massive gap between the universities where knowledge is produced and the museums where Egyptological objects are displayed. Museums are unable to catch up with the changing ethics of the discipline. In 2018, the President of the French Republic, Emmanuel Macron, announced that France would be repatriating objects looted under French colonialism to Africa.[184] However, Egyptian collections have remained, in the main, outside of Africa and, therefore, still subject to Eurocentric perspectives. This is bound to change.

Museums in Egypt once mirrored Western museums, their architecture and display echoing a Western ideology of cataloguing the museum. Today, Egypt is trying to liberate itself from cultural colonialism. Many museums are trying in their displays to defy the inherent compartmentalisation of the colonialist narrative of Egyptian heritage, which divides it into ancient Egyptian, Christian and

184. Macron 2017

Islamic; this recategorisation has been beautifully and successfully carried out in the National Museum of Civilisation, inaugurated in 2021, which has seen numbers of Egyptian visitors far greater than those in any other museum in Egypt. However, regional museums such as those in Sohag or Suez still compartmentalise the Egyptian past with displays that are marked 'Ancient Egypt', 'Christian Egypt' and 'Islamic and Modern Egypt', disregarding the historical significance of their specific geographical region, such as the importance to the Suez Museum of Abydos and Girga as well as the Suez and Red Sea regions. Neither have regional museums in Egypt, except for the Nubian and the newly inaugurated museum in Mallawi yet forged strong community relations by incorporating intangible heritage narratives. They thus maintain the colonial legacy that the museum space is reserved exclusively for the aesthetically beautiful past.

The real progress needed to safeguard the future of Egyptology starts in the classroom. Programmes teaching Egyptology are dwindling due to the lack of clear job opportunities in a competitive educational market. The core curriculum of Egyptology consists of philology (language, writing systems, epigraphy and papyrology), literature, religion and art history, taught by a restricted number of professors who have individually dominated and shaped the areas of research. Many scholars have criticised this research for its focus on the collections and archives found in such universities, which were mostly excavated from elite sites such as temples, tombs and palaces, thus favouring religion, literature and art history at the expense of history and social sciences and giving philology precedence over other analytical tools. This study of 'wonderful things' has left little opportunity for detailed theoretical, comparative, or multi-disciplinary research. As a result, Egyptology has become a rather 'isolated, conservative and bound discipline by old fashioned archaeological concerns'.[185] To face the twenty-first-century challenges confronting ancient Egypt, students of Egyptology need to be equipped with appropriate skills such as heritage studies theory and practice, politics and ethics and heritage management. Students must also have an overview of development studies, politics and anthropology. Skills in entrepreneurship and digital heritage should also be part of the preparation of Egyptologists.

A critical history of Egyptology must be written to devise a clear future. The past cannot be changed,

185. García 2014

but it can be corrected. Decolonising the historical narratives that Egyptology produces can pave the road for building proper futures for the discipline. Restitution and repatriation of the objects[186] and research archives taken under colonialism are at the heart of this liberated narrative. Reparations for past mistakes can be achieved through the restitution of agency to Egyptians to produce knowledge about their past – which can only be done with archives which remain tantalisingly out of reach. On a theoretical level, Egyptology must embrace a range of social theories more wholeheartedly to create a clearer, disciplined philosophy; Egyptology needs to look to the present as much as it looks to the past. Only this will enable Egyptology to evolve from an area of study to a more vital, rooted discipline that makes better sense to the living than the dead. Community and public archaeology must be widely practised to provide a fundamental understanding of the past through the present. International projects have in the past been guilty of foregrounding their Egyptian representatives without truly collaborating with them. Only the creation of international, truly

---

186. To join the campaign for the repatriation of the Rosetta Stone, visit www.repatriaterashid.org/; and to support the repatriation of the Bust of Nefertiti, visit www. nefertitibackhome.org/

equitable teams – rather than checking the 'Egyptian box' for a cheap photo op, or for political correctness – might go some way to saving the discipline.

Decolonising the discipline is essential, but equally important is calling out officials' post-colonial praxis in current Egyptology. Such praxis is manifested in refusing permits for community and public archaeology projects and favouring tourists who bring foreign currency above local communities. Through experience, engaging with communities and working with them is more efficient than dealing with them via a top-down approach. Research censorship, research appropriation and cultural insensitivity in Egyptological institutions have hampered the progress of the discipline into a more democratised, evolved, solid praxis.

The looting, thefts and destruction of the 2011 uprising taught us that no conservation programme, wall or security level is sufficient to protect Egyptian heritage from criminals. All these obstacles and more have imprisoned Egyptology, keeping it inaccessible to those carrying within them the intangible heritage of such a great civilisation – those who can guarantee it arrives safely in the future.

Bibliography

Abt, Jeffery. 2011. *American Egyptologist: The Life of James Henry Breasted and the Creation of His Oriental Institute*. University of Chicago Press.

Ahmed, Hussam. 2021. *The Last Nahdawi: Taha Hussein and Institution Building in Egypt*. Stanford University Press.

Ayad, M. F. 2009. *God's Wife, God's Servant: The God's Wife of Amun (ca.740–525 BC)*. Taylor & Francis.

Baines, John. 2011. 'Egyptology and the social sciences: thirty years on.' In *Methodik und Didaktik in der Ägyptologie*, 571–597. Brill Fink.

Barrowclough, David. 2016. *Digging for Hitler: The Nazi archaeologists search for an Aryan past*. Fonthill Media.

Berque, Jacques. 1972. *Egypt: Imperialism and Revolution*. London: Faber.

Blouin, Katherine, Monica Hanna and Sara Bond. 2020. 'How academics, Egyptologists, and even Melania Trump benefit from colonialist cosplay.' Hyperallergic.

Bruwier, Marie-Cécile. 1989. 'La collection égyptienne de Raoul Warocqué. 2. De 1912 à 1917.' *Les cahiers de Mariemont* 20 (1): 25–52.

Butler, Judith. 2004. *Undoing Gender*. Routledge.

2011. *Bodies That Matter: On the Discursive Limits of 'Sex'*. Taylor & Francis.

Carnarvon, George, Howard Carter and Francis Griffith. 1912. *Five Years' Explorations at Thebes: A Record of Work Done 1907–1911*. M. Martino.

Carter, Howard, and Arthur C. Mace. 2014. *The Tomb of Tutankhamun: Volume 1: Search, Discovery and Clearance of the Antechamber*. Bloomsbury Academic.

Challis, Debbie. 2013. *The Archaeology of Race: The Eugenic Ideas of Francis Galton and Flinders Petrie*. Bloomsbury Academic.

Chugg, Andrew. 2002. 'The sarcophagus of Alexander the Great?' *Greece & Rome* 49 (1): 8–26.

Colla, Elliot. 2007. *Conflicted Antiquities: Egyptology, Egyptomania, Egyptian Modernity*. e-Duke books scholarly collection: Duke University Press.

Cooney, Kara. 2018. *When Women Ruled the World: Six Queens of Egypt*. National Geographic Society.

Courrier de l'Égypte. Vol. v. 1; v. 4.

D'Athanasi, Giovanni. 1836. *A Brief Account of the Researches and Discoveries in Upper Egypt, Made Under the Direction of Henry Salt: To which is Added a Detailed Catalogue of Mr. Salt's Collection of Egyptian Antiquities*. John Hearne.

D'Auria, Sue, and Jack Josephson. 2010. *Offerings to the Discerning Eye: An Egyptological Medley in Honor of Jack A. Josephson*. Brill.

David, Elisabeth. 1999. *Gaston Maspero, 1846–1916: Le gentleman égyptologue*. Pygmalion/G. Watelet.

Davis, John. 2014. *Napoli e Napoleone: L'Italia Meridionale e le rivoluzioni europee (1780–1860)*. Rubbettino Editore.

De Beauvoir, Simone, Constance Borde and Sheila Malovany-Chevallier. 2012. *The Second Sex*. Knopf Doubleday Publishing Group.

Derby, Edward. 1864. *The Iliad of Homer, Rendered Into English Blank Verse. By Edward Earl of Derby*. Vol. v. 2: John Murray.

Derrida, Jacques, and Gayatri Spivak. 2013. *Of Grammatology*. Johns Hopkins University Press.

Djabarti, Abdelrahman, and Shmuel Moreh. 1975. *Al-Djabarti's chronicle of the first seven months of the French occupation of Egypt: muharram-rajab 1213, 15 June–December 1798: T'rîkh muddat al-faransis bi-Misr.*

DWQ (Dār al-Wathā'iq al-Qawmiyya, National Archives of Egypt). Diwan al-Madares. From the Department of Education to the Coptic Orthodox Patriarchate. 13 April 1887: 4001-000352-856.

The Foreign Affairs: al-Khārgiyya. Māṣā'il 'ilmīyah: Ḥafā'ir maqbarat Tūt 'Ankh Amūn fī Wādī al-Mulūk

Scientific Affairs: The Excavation of the Tutankhamun Tomb in Valley of the Kings. In *10/123/2*. 26 February 1923 – 17 August 1933: 0078-020312.

DWQ (Dār al-Wathā'iq al-Qawmiyya, National Archives of Egypt) al-Khārgiyya, The Foreign Affairs. Egyptologie – Donnation Rockfeller pour la creation d'un institut archeologique. 1926: 0078-034392.

Mahafez al-Abhath. Mariette Letters 1851 to 1857. In *127*: File 9.

Majlis al-Wzra' w al-Nwẓar (The Ministers' Committee). Mwzakret Nzaret al-ashghal bitalab al-tasdiq 'lā t'yyn al-Doctor burshar w al-barun Dobsing 'dwyyn fy Lajna al-āthar al-Maṣriyya (Memorandum of the Public Works Department requesting ratification of the appointment of Dr. Borchard and Baron Dobsing as members of the Egyptian Antiquities Committee). In *Mahfāza 4/3/A al-Magmū'a: 49 Ashghāl*. 25 March 1905 – 17 April 1905: Archival Code: 0075-035376.

Nizārat al-Ashghāl al-'Āmma, (Ministry of Public Works)-a. Ektarhā'āt khaasah bil-athar al-Misriyyah (Special

suggestions for the Egyptian Antiquities). In *4/2/B 692.*
23/1/1923: 0075-035363.

Nizārat al-Ashghāl al-ʿĀmma, (Ministry of Public Works)-b.
muḍakkarah min Ahmad Kamal basha'n ta'yine amīnan
bal'antikhanah ba'd istaqṣāʾ Brugsch bek min manṣabih
(Memorandum from Ahmed Kamal regarding his
appointment as secretary at the Antiquities Service after
the dismissal of Mr. Brugsch). In *Mahfāza 4/3/B 694.*
28/10/1894: 0075-035432.

The Sublime Porte, al-Māʾiyya al-Sāniya. Antiquities:
Permission to travel in the eastern and Arab regions of
Upper Egypt to Berbera with his assistants to see the ongoing
excavations in Saqqara and Al-Araba Al-Madfounda in
the provinces of Giza, Karnak, Luxor and Qurna in the
Gerga region. This is with the knowledge of the Consul
of France, Khawaja Drovetti, and to excavate some
places and take out the archaeological stones from them
and send them to Alexandria. He is not to be exposed to
the sheriffs and the overseers of the departments and all
administrators and port captains should assist him on his
way to and fro the places and to give him due honor.
In *Daftar 27.* 11 September 1828: Serial Number 349.

El Daly, Okasha. 2005. *Egyptology: The Missing Millennium.*
UCL Press.

Fagan, Brian. 2009. *The Rape of the Nile: Tomb Robbers,
Tourists, and Archaeologists in Egypt, Revised and
Updated.* Basic Books.

Fahim, Hussein. 2013. *Dams, People and Development: The
Aswan High Dam Case.* Elsevier Science.

Fahmy, Khaled. 2002. *All the Pasha's Men: Mehmed Ali, His
Army and the Making of Modern Egypt.* I. B. Tauris.

2012. *Mehmed Ali: From Ottoman Governor to Ruler of
Egypt.* Oneworld Publications.

2018. *In Quest of Justice: Islamic Law and Forensic Medicine
in Modern Egypt.* University of California Press.

Fernea, Elizabeth Warnock, Robert A. Fernea and Aleya Rouchdy. 1991. *Nubian Ethnographies*. Waveland Press.

Fernea, Robert A., and Georg Gerster. 1974. *Nubians in Egypt: Peaceful People*. University of Texas Press.

Foucault, Michel. 1982. 'The subject and power.' *Critical Inquiry* 8 (4): 777–795.

Foucault, Michel, and Jay Miskowiec. 1986. 'Of Other Spaces.' *Diacritics* 16 (1): 22.

Foucault, Michel, and Alan Sheridan. 1972. *The Archaeology of Knowledge*. Pantheon Books.

Gady, Éric. 2005. 'Le pharaon, l'égyptologue et le diplomate: les égyptologues français du voyage de Champollion à la crise de Suez (1828–1956).' Paris 4.

García, Juan Carlos Moreno. 2014. 'The Cursed Discipline?: The Peculiarities of Egyptology at the Turn of the Twenty-First Century.' In *Histories of Egyptology*, 50–63. Routledge.

Gomaà, Farouk. 1973. *Chaemwese, Sohn Ramses' II. und Hoherpriester von Memphis*. Vol. 27. Harrossowitz.

Goode, James. 2007. *Negotiating for the Past: Archaeology, Nationalism, and Diplomacy in the Middle East, 1919–1941*. University of Texas Press.

Haikal, Fayza. 2003. 'Egypt's Past Regenerated by its own People.' *Consuming Ancient Egypt*: 123.

Hamilakis, Yannis. 2014. *Archaeology and the Senses: Human Experience, Memory, and Affect*. Cambridge University Press.

Hamilakis, Yannis, Mark Pluciennik and Sarah Tarlow. 2012. *Thinking through the Body: Archaeologies of Corporeality*. Springer US.

Hamilakis, Yannis. 2005. 'Whose World and Whose Archaeology? The Colonial Present and the Return of the Political.' *Archaeologies* 1 (2): 94.

2011. 'Museums of Oblivion.' *Antiquity* 85 (328): 625.

2012. 'Are We Postcolonial Yet? Tales from the Battlefield.' *Archaeologies* 8 (1): 67. doi.org/10.1007/s11759-012-9200-5.

2016a. 'From Ethics to Politics.' In *Archaeology and Capitalism From Ethics to Politics*, edited by Philip Duke and Yannis Hamilakis.

2016b. 'Some debts can never be repaid: the archaeo-politics of the crisis.' *Journal of Modern Greek Studies* 34 (2): 227.

2018. 'Decolonial Archaeology as Social Justice.' *Antiquity* 92 (362): 518.

Hamilakis, Yannis, and Philip Duke. 2016. *Archaeology and Capitalism From Ethics to Politics*. Edited by Yannis Hamilakis. Routledge.

Hamilakis, Yannis, and Efthimis Theou. 2013. 'Enacted Multi-temporality.' *Reclaiming Archaeology: Beyond the Tropes of Modernity*. Edited by Alfredo Gonzalez-Ruibal. 181. Routledge

Hamilakis, Yannis, and Eleana Yalouri. 1996. 'Antiquities as Symbolic Capital in Modern Greek Society.' *Antiquity* 70 (267): 117.

Hanna, Monica. 2013. 'Looting in Egypt: The Unfortunate Site of Abusir el-Malek.' *Society for the Study of the Egyptian Antiquities Newsletter* 3.

2015. 'Documenting Looting Activities in Post-2011 Egypt.' In *Countering Illicit Traffic in Cultural Goods: The Global Challenge of Protecting the World's Heritage*, 47. Paris: ICOM.

2019. 'Egypt's heritage is more than an Indiana Jones movie.' *The Hill*, 2019, thehill.com/opinion/international/440035.

2020. 'Cultural Heritage Attrition in Egypt.' In *Testing the Canon of Ancient Near Eastern Art and Archaeology*, edited by Amy Rebecca Gansell and Ann Shafer, 318. Oxford University Press.

2021. 'Women are from Africa and men are from Europe.' In *The Routledge Companion to Black Women's Cultural Histories*, 13–22. Routledge.

2022. 'Repatriating Cultural Identity: The Egyptian Discontinuity Pretext.' In *Museums, Transculturality, and the*

Nation-State: Case Studies from a Global Context, edited by Leeb Susanne and Samuel Nina, 87–102. transcript Verlag.

2023. 'Contesting the Lonely Queen.' *Journal of Cultural Property*: 1–19.

Harrison, Rodney. 2012. *Heritage: Critical Approaches*. Routledge.

Hodder, Ian. 1992. 'The domestication of Europe.' In *Theory and practice in archaeology*, edited by Ian Hodder, 241. Routledge.

Hodder, Ian. 1995. *Theory and Practice in Archaeology*. Second edn. Routledge.

2006. *Çatalhöyük: the leopard's tale: revealing the mysteries of Turkey's ancient 'town'*. London: Thames & Hudson.

2012a. *Entangled: An Archaeology of the Relationships between Humans and Things*. Wiley.

2012b. *The Present Past: An Introduction to Anthropology for Archeologists*. Pen & Sword Archaeology.

2016. *Studies in Human-thing Entanglement*.

Hodder, Ian, and Scott Hutson. 2003. *Reading the Past: Current Approaches to Interpretation in Archaeology*. Cambridge University Press.

Howley, Kathryn, and Rune Nyord. 2018. 'Editorial Introduction-Egyptology and Anthropology: Historiography, Theoretical Exchange, and Conceptual Development.' *Journal of Ancient Egyptian Interconnections* 17.

Iggers, Georg, Edward Wang and Supriya Mukherjee. 2013. *A Global History of Modern Historiography*. Taylor & Francis.

Ikram, Salima, and Monica Hanna. 2013. 'Looting and land grabbing: the current situation in Egypt.' *ARCE Bulletin* 202: 34.

Iskin, Ruth. 2022. 'The Other Nefertiti: Symbolic Restitutions.' *Contested Holdings: Museum Collections in Political, Epistemic and Artistic Processes of Return* 14: 65–78.

Jach, Anthoni. 2007. *Napoleon's Double*. Giramondo.

James, T. G. H. 2006. *Howard Carter: The path to Tutankhamun*. London: Tauris Parke.

Jarus, Owen. 2016. 'Blood & Gold: Children Dying As Egypt's Treasures Are Looted.' Livescience. Last Modified 8 August 2016. www.livescience.com/55687-children-dying-in-egypt-looting.html.

Joyce, Rosemary A. 2004. 'Embodied subjectivity: gender, femininity, masculinity, sexuality.' *A companion to social archaeology*: 82.

Joyce, Rosemary A., and Lynn M. Meskell. 2014. *Embodied Lives: Figuring Ancient Maya and Egyptian Experience*. Routledge.

Jurman, Claus. 2022. 'Pharaoh's new clothes.' *On (post) colonial Egyptology, hypocrisy, and the elephant in the room. DOI* 10.

Kamil, Jill. 2007. *Labib Habachi: The Life and legacy of an Egyptologist*. Amercain University in Cairo Press.

Kawai, Nozomu. 2013. 'Khaemwaset.' *The Encyclopedia of Ancient History*.

Kelley, Robin D. G. 1992. An archaeology of resistance. JSTOR.

Kenawi, Mohamed. 2024. 'What is Happening to Egyptian Heritage?: The Case of Privately Owned Buildings.' In *The Routledge Handbook of Heritage Destruction*, 357-371. Routledge.

Khaldūn, Ibn, and Charles Issawi. 1992. *An Arab philosophy of history: selections from the Prolegomena of Ibn Khaldun of Tunis (1332–1406)*. Vol. Book, Whole. Cairo: American University in Cairo Press.

Khaldûn, Ibn Khaldun, N.J. Dawood, Franz Rosenthal, and B.B. Lawrence. 2020. *The Muqaddimah: An Introduction to History – Abridged Edition*. Princeton University Press.

Kiffer, André. 2019. *Battle of Ayn Jalut, September 3rd, 1260*.

Kleinitz, Cornelia, and Claudia Näser. 2011. 'The loss of innocence: political and ethical dimensions of the Merowe

Dam Archaeological Salvage Project at the Fourth Nile Cataract (Sudan).' *Conservation and Management of Archaeological sites* 13 (2-3): 253-280.

2012. ' *Nihna Nas Al-bahar- We are the People of the River.':* *Ethnographic Research in the Fourth Nile Cataract Region, Sudan.* Vol. 26. Harrassowitz.

2013. 'Archaeology, development and conflict: a case study from the African continent.' *Archaeologies* 9: 162–191.

Langer, Christian, and Uroš Matić. 2023. 'Postcolonial Theory in Egyptology: Key Concepts and Agendas.' *Archaeologies* 19 (1): 1–27.

Langer, Christian, M Woons, and S Weier. 2017. 'The informal colonialism of Egyptology: from the French expedition to the security state.' *Critical epistemologies of global politics.*

Lemos, Rennan. 2023. 'Can We Decolonize the Ancient Past? Bridging Postcolonial and Decolonial Theory in Sudanese and Nubian Archaeology.' *Cambridge Archaeological Journal* 33 (1): 19-37. https://doi.org/10.1017/S0959774322000178. https://www.cambridge.org/core/article/can-we-decolonize-the-ancient-past-bridging-postcolonial-and-decolonial-theory-in-sudanese-and-nubian-archaeology/D5CDDC7D319DEB339A26FAC765245C2D.

The Letters of the Officers of the French Army. 1801. The British Library.

Lichtheim, Miriam. 1973. *Ancient Egyptian Literature: The Old and Middle Kingdoms.* University of California Press.

Macron, Emmanuel. 2017. Discourt d'Emmanuel Macron à l'université de Ouagadougou. Burkina Faso.

Marchant, Jo. 2011. 'Archaeology meets politics: Spring comes to ancient Egypt.' *Nature* 479 (7374): 464–467.

Matić, Uroš. 2012. 'To queer or not to queer? That is the question: sex/gender, prestige and burial no. 10 on the Mokrin necropolis.' *Dacia NS* 56: 169–185.

2016. 'Gender in Ancient Egypt: Norms, Ambiguities, and Sensualities.' *Near Eastern Archaeology* 79 (3): 174-183. https://doi.org/10.5615/neareastarch.79.3.0174. https://www.journals.uchicago.edu/doi/abs/10.5615/neareastarch.79.3.0174.

2023.'Postcolonialism as a Reverse Discourse in Egyptology: De-colonizing Historiography and Archaeology of Ancient Egypt and Nubia Part 2.' *Archaeologies* 19 (1): 60–82.

Mayes, Stanley. 2003. *The Great Belzoni: The Circus Strongman Who Discovered Egypt's Ancient Treasure.* Bloomsbury USA.

Mazis, Glen. 1992. 'Merleau-Ponty and the Backward Flow of Time: The Reversibility of Temporality and the Temporality of Reversibility,' in Shaun Gallagher Thomas Busch (ed.), *Merleau-Ponty, Hermeneutics and Postmodernism*

Merleau-Ponty, Maurice. 1962. *Phenomenology of Perception Phénoménologie de la Perception.* Routledge and Kegan Paul.

Meskell, Lynn. 1991. *Archaeologies of Social Life: Age, Sex, Class Etcetra in Ancient Egypt.* Wiley.

2018. *A Future in Ruins: UNESCO, World Heritage, and the Dream of Peace.* Oxford University Press.

Mickel, Allison. 2021. *Why Those Who Shovel Are Silent: A History of Local Archaeological Knowledge and Labor.* University Press of Colorado.

Millet, Pierre, and Stanislas Millet. 1903. *Le Chasseur Pierre Millet: Souvenirs de la campagne d'Égypte 1798–1801; Avec introd., notes et app.* E.-Paul.

Moser, Stephanie, Darren Glazier, James E. Phillips, Lamya Nasser el Nemr, Mohammed Saleh Mousa, Rascha Nasr Aiesh, Susan Richardson, Andrew Conner, and Michael Seymour. 2002. 'Transforming archaeology through practice: Strategies for collaborative archaeology and the Community Archaeology Project at Quseir, Egypt.' *World Archaeology* 34 (2): 220. https://doi.org/10.1080/ 0043824022000007071. https://doi.org/10.1080/00438 24022000007071.

Napoleon I, Emperor of the French, M. Jomard, Marie Jules Ce sar Lelorgne de Savigny, and Jean Baptiste Joseph baron Fourier. 1809. *Description de l'Egypte: ou, Recueil des observations et des recherches qui ont ete faites en Egypte pendant l'expedition de l'armee francaise*. Paris: Impr. impériale.

Neugebauer, Otto. 2012. *A history of ancient mathematical astronomy*. Vol. 1. Springer Science & Business Media.

Noury, Rizk. 2018. *Qāwānyn wa lawaʾih al-aṯār al-miṣrīyyah (min ʿasr Muḥammad ʿAlī ḥatta thawrat Yūlyū 1952)*. Edited by Ahmed el-Shoky. Cairo: Dār al-Wathāʾiq al-Qawmiyya, National Archives of Egypt.

Parkinson, Richard. 2005. *The Rosetta Stone*. British Museum Press.

Parkinson, Richard B. 2009. *Reading ancient Egyptian poetry: among other histories*. John Wiley & Sons.

Pawly, Ronald, and Patrice Courcelle. 2012. *Napoleon's Mamelukes*. Bloomsbury Publishing.

Pennington, Benjamin T., Penelope Wilson, Fraser Sturt and Antony G. Brown. 2020. 'Landscape change in the Nile Delta during the fourth millennium BC: A new perspective on the Egyptian Predynastic and Protodynastic periods.' *World Archaeology* 52 (4): 550–565.

Petrie, William Matthew Flinders. 2013. *Seventy years in archaeology*. Cambridge University Press.

Piacentini, Patrizia. 2021. 'Italy.' In *A History of World Egyptology*, edited by Aidan Dodson and Salima Ikram Andrew Bednarski. Cambridge: Cambridge University Press.

Quirke, Stephen. 2013. 'Exclusion of Egyptians in English-directed archaeology 1882–1922 under British occupation of

Egypt.' Ägyptologen und Ägyptologien zwischen Kaiserreich und gründung der beiden Deutschen staaten: Reflexionen zur geschichte und episteme eines altertumswissenschaftlichen fachs im 150 jahr der Zeitschrift für Ägyptische Sprache und Altertumskunde: 379–406.

Reid, Donald. 1985. 'Indigenous Egyptology: The Decolonization of a Profession?' *Journal of the American Oriental Society* 105 (2): 233–246.

2003. *Whose Pharaohs?: Archaeology, Museums, and Egyptian National Identity from Napoleon to World War I*. University of California Press.

2015. *Contesting Antiquity in Egypt: Archaeologies, Museums, and the Struggle for Identities from World War I to Nasser*. American University in Cairo Press.

Renfrew, C., and P. Bahn. 2020. *Archaeology: Theories, Methods and Practice*. Thames & Hudson.

Ricci, Alessandro, and Daniele Salvoldi. 2018. *From Siena to Nubia: Alessandro Ricci in Egypt and Sudan, 1817–22*. American University in Cairo Press.

Riggs, Christina. 2021. *Treasured: How Tutankhamun Shaped a Century*. Atlantic Books.

Said, Edward. 1995. *Orientalism*. Penguin.

Said, Edward W. 1975. 'Chomsky and the Question of Palestine.' *Journal of Palestine Studies* 4 (3): 91–104.

Sayce, Archibald Henry. 1923. *Reminiscences*. Macmillan.

Sayyid-Marsot, Afaf. 1969. *Egypt and Cromer: A Study in Anglo-Egyptian Relations*. Praeger.

2007. *A History of Egypt: From the Arab Conquest to the Present*. Cambridge University Press.

Seton-Thompson, Grace. 1923. *A Woman Tenderfoot in Egypt*. Dodd, Mead.

Shanks, Michael, and Christopher Tilley. 1996. *Social Theory and Archaeology*. Polity Press.

Spriggs, Matthew. 1984. *Marxist Perspectives in Archaeology*. Cambridge University Press.

Strathern, Paul. 2008. *Napoleon in Egypt*. Random House.

Thompson, J. 2015a. *Wonderful Things: A History of Egyptology*. 2: *The Golden Age: 1881–1914*. American University in Cairo Press.

Thompson, Jason. 2015b. *Wonderful Things: A History of Egyptology*. Volume II: American University in Cairo Press.

2018. *Wonderful Things: A History of Egyptology*. 3: *From 1914 to the twenty-first century*. American University in Cairo Press.

Thompson, Jason, and Jaromir Malek. 2020. *Wonderful Things: A History of Egyptology*. 1: *from Antiquity To 1881*. American University in Cairo Press.

Tilley, Christopher. 1990. *Michel Foucault: towards an archaeology of archaeology*.

1997. *A Phenomenology of Landscape: Places, Paths and Monuments*. Berg Publishers.

2014. *Material Culture and Text: The Art of Ambiguity*. Taylor & Francis.

2020. *The Materiality of Stone: Explorations in Landscape Phenomenology*. Taylor & Francis.

Tully, Gemma, and Monica Hanna. 2013. 'One landscape, many tenants: Uncovering multiple claims, visions and meanings on the Theban necropolis.' *Archaeologies* 9 (3): 362.

Van Der Spek, Kees. 2008. 'Faked Antikas and "Modern Antiques": The production and marketing of tourist art in the Theban Necropolis.' *Journal of Social Archaeology* 8 (2): 162–189.

2011. *The Modern Neighbors of Tutankhamun: History, Life, and Work in the Villages of the Theban West Bank*. American University in Cairo Press.

Vercoutter, J., and C. Vandersleyen. 1992. *L'Egypte et la vallée du Nil: De la fin de l'Ancien Empire à la fin du Nouvel Empire*. Presses universitaires de France.

Waddell, William. 2018. *Delphi Complete Works of Manetho (Illustrated)*. Delphi Classics.

Weeks, Kent R., and Manfred Bietak. 1979. *Egyptology and the social sciences: five studies*. Cairo: American University in Cairo Press.

Weiss, Lara. 2022. *The Walking Dead at Saqqara: Strategies of Social and Religious Interaction in Practice*. De Gruyter.

Welch, William. 1988. *No Country For A Gentleman: British Rule in Egypt, 1883–1907*. Bloomsbury Academic.

Wilkinson, Toby. 2012. *Royal Annals of Ancient Egypt*. London: Kegan Paul International.

Wilson, John. 1964. *Signs and wonders upon Pharaoh: a history of American Egyptology*. publisher not identified.

Yusuf, Ahmed Abdelhamid, and Fayza Haikal. 2003. *From Pharaoh's Lips*. American University in Cairo Press.

Acknowledgments

I want to thank my husband Daniele and daughter Maya, who skipped many family events and outings to help me write and stay focused. I especially want to thank my brother Michael, who pulled me through the final stretch of writing, and my brother Bishoy, whose great sense of humour always helped me. I want to thank my parents, Amany and Samir, for their continuous encouragement and support. I want to thank the College of Archaeology and Cultural Heritage team at the Arab Academy for Science and Technology, who supported me through the process. I am also thankful to all my students for their great discussions, insights and inspiration. I particularly want to thank researchers Habiba Abdelnaby and Hassan Abo el-Nasr, who provided great help with data collection. Finally, I want to thank my editor, Tom Clayton, whose unmatched patience and support made this book possible.

About the Series

Each volume in the FUTURES Series presents a vision imagined by an accomplished writer and subject expert. The series seeks to publish a diverse range of voices, covering as wide-ranging a view as possible of our potential prospects. Inspired by the brilliant 'To-Day and To-Morrow' books from a century ago, we ask our authors to write in a spirit of pragmatic hope, and with a commitment to map out potential future landscapes, highlighting both beauties and dangers. We hope the books in the FUTURES Series will inspire readers to imagine what might lie ahead, to figure out how they might like the future to look, and, indeed, to think about how we might get there.

The FUTURES Series was originally conceived by Professor Max Saunders and Dr Lisa Gee, both of whom work at the University of Birmingham. Saunders is Interdisciplinary Professor of Modern Literature and Culture, author of *Imagined Futures: Writing, Science, and Modernity in the To-Day and To-Morrow book series*, 1923–31 (OUP 2019), and editor of *The To-day and To-morrow Reader* (Routledge, 2024), and Gee is Assistant Professor in Creative Writing and Digital Media and Research Fellow in Future Thinking.

To find out more about their Future Thinking work visit www.birmingham.ac.uk/futures

Also available in the FUTURES Series: